POWERHOUSE PARTNERS

Powerhouse
Partners

A BLUEPRINT for BUILDING
ORGANIZATIONAL CULTURE
for BREAKAWAY RESULTS

STEPHEN M. DENT and JAMES H. KREFFT

Davies-Black Publishing
Palo Alto, California

Published by Davies-Black Publishing, a division of CPP, Inc., 3803 East Bayshore Road, Palo Alto, CA 94303; 800-624-1765.

Special discounts on bulk quantities of Davies-Black books are available to corporations, professional associations, and other organizations. For details, contact the Director of Marketing and Sales at Davies-Black Publishing; 650-691-9123; fax 650-623-9271.

Visit the Davies-Black Publishing web site at www.davies-black.com.

08 07 06 05 04   10 9 8 7 6 5 4 3 2 1
Printed in the United States of America

Library of Congress Cataloging-in-Publication Data
Dent, Stephen M.
    Powerhouse partners : a blueprint for building organizational culture for breakaway results / Stephen M. Dent & James H. Krefft.—1st ed.
        p. cm.
    Includes bibliographical references and index.
    ISBN 0-89106-195-9 (hardcover)
    1. Strategic alliances (Business) 2. Business networks. 3. Corporate culture.
        I. Krefft, James H. II. Title.
    HD69.S8D468 2004
    658' .044—dc22
                                                                                    2004013379
FIRST EDITION
First printing 2004

This book is dedicated to working men and women everywhere. Your creativity, agility, and resiliency have elevated human-kind and benefited countless numbers of people in achieving a happier, healthier, and more prosperous life.

—STEPHEN M. DENT

To my wife, Lynn, and to our children, Michelle and Jim, for being there when I needed them, and for not being there when I needed to be alone at the keyboard.

—JAMES H. KREFFT

Contents

Acknowledgments   xi
About the Authors   xiii
Introduction: An End, a Beginning   1

Chapter 1. Coming Full Circle with Organization Culture   9
Chapter 2. Building a Partnering Organization   21

THE POWERHOUSE PARTNER MODEL

Chapter 3. Shaping Your Culture with the Powerhouse
Partner Model   39

STEP 1: Practice Focused Leadership

Chapter 4. Attaining Personal Mastery, Inspiring Vision,
Motivating Action, Achieving Results   51

STEP 2: Build a Partnering Infrastructure

Chapter 5. Redesigning Your Organization As a
Partnering Network   59
Chapter 6. Hiring People with Partnering Competencies   85
Chapter 7. Keeping and Growing Smart Partners   111

STEP 3: Develop Smart Partners

Chapter 8. Reinforcing the Foundation for Openness   133
Chapter 9. Moving to the Future with Creativity   157
Chapter 10. Embracing Connectivity for Agility   183

Conclusion: Working Toward Resiliency   203
Bibliography   221
Index   227

Acknowledgments

A special thanks goes out to James H. Krefft, Ph.D., co-author of this book. His dedication, intelligence, and insights have contributed greatly to the development of these concepts. I want to thank my clients—American Medical Association, Bank of America, Exult Inc., GMAC-RFC, Minnesota Department of Transportation, NASA, Wells Fargo Bank, and Xcel Energy, to name a few—who have greatly contributed to the growing body of knowledge on the importance of building people's Partnering Intelligence and a partnering culture. I especially want to acknowledge and thank my colleagues at Partnership Continuum, Inc., for their loyalty and hard work in building on this body of knowledge and putting it into practical applications every day. Special recognition goes to Neal R. Holtan, M.D., M.P.H., and Phyl Burger for their support. Many thanks to Laurie Harper, our literary agent, and the staff at CPP, Inc./Davies-Black Publishing for making all of this look so easy. Finally, to honor the memory of my dear friend, colleague, and mentor, Jerry Martin, who worked with me to develop the underpinning theories of Partnering Intelligence. Thank you, dear friend.

—STEPHEN M. DENT

I want to thank my colleague Stephen Dent for generously inviting me to collaborate on *Powerhouse Partners*. Special appreciation goes to Laurie Harper, our agent, who helped us tighten the focus of the book and went to extremes to get it sold in an uncertain market. Thanks to the many clients from whom I have learned in practical ways the power of partnering, especially Peter Cahn of ExxonMobil,

Lionel Ferguson (formerly of GE Capital), Beth Mackay of Perot Systems, Steve Sargent of GE Capital, Kevin Wild of Qwest Wireless, and Jim McNulty, Tim Melson, and Ronn Williamson (all formerly of Thermo King). Singular gratitude goes to my wife, Lynn, for supporting me without limits and to my children, Michelle and Jim, whose own blossoming skills as writers continually push me to improve my own writing.

—JAMES H. KREFFT

About the Authors

Stephen M. Dent is a pioneer in Partnering Intelligence theory, research, and application, the culmination of more than twenty-five years of experience helping companies improve performance through leadership, partnership, and employee development. He is an internationally known author, lecturer, and consultant, and the founder of Partnership Continuum, Inc., a Minneapolis-based consultancy delivering partnering and leadership excellence to diverse organizations worldwide.

James H. Krefft, Ph.D., consults with organizations in implementing large-scale change. With international experience in the formulation of strategic direction, organization design, competency-based selection, and human performance systems, he has enabled client organizations such as Department of Energy, ExxonMobil, GE Capital, Pinnacle West Capital, Qwest Wireless, and Thermo King to exceed revenue goals and to save over $1.8 billion, collectively. In addition to co-authoring *Powerhouse Partners,* he has published articles and case studies on implementing large-scale organizational changes and is co-writing a book on how to redefine retirement.

Introduction:
An End, a Beginning

Scarcely anything material or established which I was brought up to believe was permanent and vital, has lasted. Everything I was sure or taught to be sure was impossible, has happened.

—WINSTON CHURCHILL, *MY EARLY LIFE*

People once instinctively understood and practiced the art of connectivity—to the land, to nature, and to each other. As human cultures evolved, we slowly forgot the basic partnering skills that allowed us to survive ice ages and other hostile planetary environments. From simple organisms to complex organizations, nature has instilled lessons that businesses must relearn if they are to thrive in the new economic environment of the digital age. People survive and grow by propagating connections to each other, to the world around us. In today's economic environment connectivity is critical for any business to become a true *Powerhouse Partner.*

We knew it before the wheel, before agriculture, before cave paintings. For millennia people have recognized and appreciated the value of partnering. Long ago we learned that to survive we needed to work together and be loyal to one another. We succeeded as hunters and gatherers and shared in the bounty yielded by our willingness to partner and commit to one another. In those early days trust was everything because failing to trust companions, or deceiving them in any way, could result in starvation. It was as simple as that. Greed might shake the tribe, but disloyalty would shatter it. Connections formed the foundation of civilization and accelerated our ascendancy as a species. However, our progress has often been thwarted by our moving one step forward and two steps back. One of the principal causes of our connections beginning to unravel was the introduction of "scientific" approaches to management. Call it "workplace rationalism."

During the Age of Enlightenment, philosophers, scientists, and other scholars began to take stuff apart to understand better how the universe works. Like tinkering three-year-olds tugging on the loose threads of a sock, these academics began to yank at the connections that linked people together. Metaphysicians struggled to dissect the unseeable, physicians dismembered cadavers, and physicists sliced and diced particles in a quest for the building blocks of matter—and life. Disconnection seemed to proffer stepping-stones to enlightenment. Pulling on threads supplied us with answers to gnawing questions. What are the nine orders of angels? How does adrenalin drive our behavior? Why does a boson have zero or integral spin? Yet the truth, it appeared, was always but one more layer down or deep. But like Peer Gynt in Ibsen's play, we will forever be frustrated in our search for an onion's core.

With the Industrial Age, the scientific discipline of disconnecting assaulted the workplace. Breaking out and isolating individual processes and tasks drove industrial productivity. Control of material resources and specialization set the stage for a scarcity mentality. In the Industrial Age, access to raw materials drove imperialism as nations saw their own reserves depleted and sought control over new resources in distant lands. Nations went to war over rights to dig mines, establish plantations, and clear-cut forests. But that era of scarcity is rapidly being eclipsed by the surging vigor of the digital age. Information has become the primary source of production, and hot links are everywhere. Human societies and technologies are now linked and overlap in complex and unexpected ways. Thai rice farmers talk to their families via wireless telephone from their fields, while Mexican auto manufacturing managers download the latest technical schematic from their design center in Germany.

This ever-thickening gumbo of cultural and technical integration calls for business leaders to rethink the models they have been using to manage their enterprises. In today's culturally complex and technically intricate, nothing-ever-stays-the-same-for-very-long global marketplace, organization leaders can no longer use governance and management models based on twentieth-century military-industrial architectures, hierarchies designed more to disconnect than to connect. Hierarchies restrict movement, limit speed, exert control, and deflect risk. Like our nomadic ancestors who banded together to hunt and gather, we must relearn the art, the skills, and the power of connectivity.

SMART PARTNERING

To survive, we must partner. To thrive, we must become smart partners. The sphere of "me" is collapsing in on itself as businesses slowly migrate from hierarchical to networking organizations. Successful leaders must understand and appreciate the profound marketplace implications of this human journey from connections to disconnections to reconnections. Businesses are becoming organic networks, neural webs. Networks grow by propagating connections. Connectivity happens when businesses form strategic alliances and partnerships within and between themselves. Alliances produce astonishing results only when information flows freely and people trust each other and are loyal to one another.

Organizations are struggling to react quickly to ever-changing customer needs, alliances, technologies, and top-talent wants and whims. Companies are straining to shift with market winds and financial swings, striving to outlast competitors. Openness, agility, creativity, and resiliency are needed to stay afloat in shifting currents. Smart partnering, and the ability to create a partnering culture invigorated by the partnering infrastructure needed to focus on rapidly changing situations, will enable business leaders to relearn this ancient art and translate it into a modern business model. As customer needs swirl, as markets migrate, as technologies erupt, as a new generation bursts into the American workforce, as partners tango and split up and dance again, companies must have a superabundance of connections to withstand the shockwaves of these massive movements. Like the age of machines waltzed in the Industrial Age, the information age now dances with a partner, the age of connections. Information fuels connections, and connections create new information. Call our time the *Dual Age of Information and Connections.*

The ability to partner successfully in the Dual Age of Information and Connections has an impact on every aspect of an organization's culture and operations—from its strategic framework, through its business processes, to its human resources strategy—resulting in a workplace where people want to stay and to which they will contribute their best talents. Building on the Partnership Continuum™ partnering model first proposed by Stephen M. Dent in *Partnering Intelligence: Creating Value for Your Business by Building Strong Alliances* (1999, 2004), Powerhouse Partners provides readers with an organization model designed for fast-forward businesses that understand the value of connectivity and loyalty. The Powerhouse Partner Model offers the structure and skills needed to build a partnering infrastructure while inspiring employee loyalty and commitment to the vision and objectives of the enterprise. Powerhouse Partners shows you in practical ways how to transition from a traditional enterprise to a partnering organization.

CREATING A PARTNERING CULTURE

Chapter 1, an overview of organization culture, underscores the link between culture and bottom-line business results. An organization culture is a self-reinforcing system, and culture rules. Culture springs mainly from how leaders behave. *Culture by evolution* happens when no deliberate thought or design is applied to the configuration of an organization's culture. *Culture by design* happens when leaders sit down and formulate a culture and then rigorously communicate and live by its tenets. In the twenty-first century, a business that wants to stay alive, and thrive, must learn the lessons of a designed culture.

After opening with some key culture-related questions, Chapter 2 outlines the authors' concept of a partnering organization and lists its advantages as compared to a traditional command-and-control enterprise. To build a partnering organization, leaders must create a partnering culture, a culture designed both to expedite internal alliances and to extend the same partnering expertise externally to forge mutually beneficial relationships with other companies. The primary characteristics of a partnering culture derive from the Six Partnering Attributes™: Self-Disclosure and Feedback, Win-Win

Orientation, Ability to Trust, Future Orientation, Comfort with Change, and Comfort with Interdependence. A partnering culture, a governing culture, fosters collaboration among existing subcultures, rather than cutthroat competition. Creating a partnering culture positions an organization to accrue four chief benefits: openness, creativity, agility, and resiliency.

INTRODUCING THE POWERHOUSE PARTNER MODEL

In the Dual Age of Information and Connections, creating the value and innovation needed to move an organization to the next level requires a focused effort on harnessing and releasing human potential and creativity. But how? Chapter 3 presents the Powerhouse Partner Model, a blueprint for building a partnering powerhouse, comprising three components:

- Practicing focused leadership

- Building a partnering infrastructure

- Developing smart partners

These three inputs combine to create a partnering culture, the foundation of a partnering organization. Strong leaders build healthy cultures. In practicing focused leadership, leaders start with themselves, purposefully committing to behave in an open and trusting manner by using the interpersonal skills described in the Six Partnering Attributes. The second step in creating a partnering culture is to be sure the organization's infrastructure supports a collaborative culture. The third step is to strengthen partnering behaviors in the organization, creating a self-reinforcing network and embedding partnering language and behaviors deeper and deeper within the organization.

Organization culture changes one person at a time. Leaders have a critical role in the process, and it starts with having an accurate assessment of one's own capabilities. Chapter 4 explores the components of personal mastery in using the Six Partnering Attributes, inspiring vision and motivating others to achieve more than the mundane.

If partnering is emerging as an essential business strategy for the Dual Age of Information and Connections, what are the implications of embracing a partnering philosophy on the structure of an organization? To help answer that question, Chapter 5 gets into the nuts and bolts of job and organization design. The chapter introduces the job design concepts of a Partnering Profile and a Partnering Summary and the organization design model of a partnering network that is focused and aligned to achieve the enterprise's strategic framework: its vision, mission, and strategic directions. Partnering creates value; people partner; build your organization for partnering; pay for partnering. Partnering creates value, and it's people who partner. Therefore, you must construct an organization to enable partnering to happen and reward people for partnering. In sum, the chapter provides practical ideas for how to institutionalize partnering in the Dual Age of Information and Connections.

But what does a smart partner look like? Chapter 6 recommends that companies rethink the competencies they view as core to their organization's culture and success. Partnering-enabling competencies must form the foundation for an organization's human performance system in the Dual Age of Information and Connections. Also introduced in this chapter is the concept of a Partnering Interview, a proprietary, innovative approach for determining the breadth and depth of a job candidate's partnering competencies. A Partnering Interview Plan is a tool that interviewers can use to note critical questions to ask and to ensure that interviewers probe all relevant partnering competencies.

Smart partners drive creativity by increasing the frequency, frankness, and fruitfulness of interpersonal connections, dialogue, and collaboration. Chapter 7 proposes three concrete action steps an organization's leaders can take to keep and grow smart partners in the twenty-first century: build loyalty and a sense of duty; coach people to grow informal communication networks (pathways); and strengthen relationship skills. Relationship skills are required both for leaders, to manage a new kind of diversity—one of opinions and ideas and approaches to processing information—and for employees, to enable them not only to tolerate such diversity of perspectives, but also to cherish it as the fuel of creativity.

The foundation of a culture is how people communicate with each other and whether they believe the communication will be followed up with actions consistent with the communication. When people do not trust each other, they typically hold information close to the vest. Chapter 8 tackles reinforcing the foundation for the organizational openness required for people to trust each other and to share information. A partnering culture encourages self-disclosure and feedback. Without accurate information about a trading partner's needs and wants, the success of any marketplace exchange falls largely to chance. Smart partnering helps you see what is happening in the marketplace with a fresh perspective. Trust forms the foundation of a work climate in which people know and appreciate the limits of reliability and can be sure that these borders will be respected. Only one experience of betrayal will threaten even the best-crafted partnership.

Businesses today are facing a colossal transformation in the marketplace. One key to making the kinds of cultural adaptations needed to survive, even thrive, in the twenty-first century is linked to a leader's capacity not only to think about the future, but also to live in the future. Chapter 9 addresses moving to the future with creativity. In a partnering culture, creativity comes about most directly from having a future orientation and being comfortable with change. Bonded together, they form a sturdy platform for creativity and innovation. If a business has a past orientation, it tends to impose past experience on new situations. With a future orientation, it is more likely to see the possibilities in new situations and approach them with hope and good faith. Finding a level of comfort with change enables an organization to identify obstacles to change, develop strategies for coping with them, and formulate action plans for implementing desired business changes.

In the Dual Age of Information and Connections, businesses by necessity must reach out, form new business relationships, profit from them, and move on quickly. Businesses must propagate connections. Chapter 10 explores embracing connectivity for agility. In a partnering culture, a win-win orientation forms the bedrock of marketplaces. Interconnections among marketplaces give an organization ready access to competencies and resources it does not possess in-house. Links build agility. Interdependence in particular enables continuity and vibrancy in marketplaces. Interdependence is an active, ongoing process that requires all parties to move apace from initial independence to vibrant collaboration. It serves as the foundation of the marketplace component of organization culture. Forget about getting a bigger slice of the pie—partner to make the pie bigger and sweeter.

BE A POWERHOUSE PARTNER

In today's culturally complex global marketplace, leaders can no longer depend on governance models based on twentieth-century management architectures, hierarchies designed more to disconnect than to connect. In the conclusion we summarize how all six competencies of a partnering organization—corresponding to the Six Partnering Attributes—work together to produce resiliency, to create a Powerhouse Partner. To sustain itself, to adjust continually to changes beyond its control, to see what others do not, and to capitalize on those insights, an organization must be imbued thoroughly with all six attributes. Cultures that have been designed to champion a powerful purpose stand the test of time. Smart partnering, and the ability to create a partnering culture invigorated by the partnering infrastructure needed to adapt to rapidly changing situations, will enable business leaders to relearn the ancient art of connection and translate it into a modern business model.

Smart partners win not only because of what they do, but also because of how they do it. Powerhouse Partners know how to do four things well:

- Keep their eye on the ball

- Promote openness and embrace a diversity of ideas and approaches for processing information

- Approach the marketplace with an abundance mentality and foster the organization changes needed to keep pace with the marketplace

- Leverage connectedness and appreciate the value of building the relationship skills needed to forge enduring partnerships, internally and externally

The organizations that do these four things the best will become the Powerhouse Partners of the Dual Age of Information and Connections.

1

Coming Full Circle with Organization Culture

In America: "Time is money."
In Belarus: "Time costs nothing."

Western culture traces a path of survival from hunter-gatherers through agrarian societies, city-states, nation-states, the Age of Enlightenment, the Industrial Age, and the beckoning Dual Age of Information and Connections. Our nomadic ancestors understood the value of working in partnership with each other for the tribe's survival. As people settled down, we became less concerned with our neighbors' survival and more concerned about ourselves. This trend toward disconnection was reinforced through scientific methodologies. In effect, "me" became more important than "we." However, as we move into a new organic economic structure, remembering past survival lessons—such as the importance of con-nectivity, alignment, loyalty, and trust—will ensure smart organiza-tions a long, prosperous life in the twenty-first century.

Organizations experience the same needs, threats, and life cycles as other species. Organizations are born, grow, wither, and die. They frequently produce offspring, sometimes on purpose and more often by accident. Organizations are more like you and I than not. And conversely, in many ways we are what we organize. An organization's environment plays a vital role in nourishing it—or menacing it. When environmental conditions change dramatically, trigger-ing a climate hostile to life, the inhabitants need to adapt, flee, or

die. During the last ice age, many people died as the northern popu-
lations of Europe retreated to the warmer environs of Iberia, the
Balkans, and Ukraine. The harsh environment to the north no
longer fostered human life, and the remaining inhabitants fled to
survive.

In addition to influencing the well-being of individuals, the environment shapes the nuances of the cultures that develop within it.
People who live in tropical ecosystems, for example, have cultures
different from residents of subarctic environs. They dress differently,
view time differently, eat differently, and play differently. These
behavioral adaptations result from the natural laws that influence
how people interact with each other. People are fettered by these
natural laws in extraordinary and complex ways. In some African
cultures along the equator, for example, food-gathering strategies
were based on what was ripe during a particular season and har-
vested as needed. In northern European tribes, where winter wreaked
havoc on native food-bearing plants, organized groups of people
sowed, collected, and stored food for the winter. These different
strategies, driven by dissimilar environmental conditions, molded the
development of cultures in those places. But regardless of the set
of strategies employed, each tribal group wove itself intricately
into the natural fabric around them, observed and learned how to
maneuver within that microenvironment, and created or adapted
strategies for survival. The environment helps define almost every
aspect of our personal, family, and community lives—and our formal
organizations.

It may not appear that ancestral survival habits have much to do
with organizations in the twenty-first century, but we can and need
to learn from them. The environments that exist around and within
an organization—whether it is a little league team, a monastic community, or a Fortune 500 corporation—govern how successful it is
likely to be. How the members of an organization behave, the norms
within which they function, and how they link to one another all
flow out of its environment. Organizations that understand the
connectivity of their success to internal and external environments
will have competitive advantages over those that do not make the
connection.

ORGANIZATION CULTURE
AND THE BOTTOM LINE

When we speak about environment in this context, what we are talking about is the culture of an organization. Culture sums up what we believe and what we disavow, what we cherish and what we scorn, what we say and what we do not say, what we do and what we do not do. In short, culture is "how things are done around here." It's how we act, or not. Every organization has a culture, often an amalgam of many subcultures, each subculture being driven by its own history, needs, motivation, successes, and failures. The ties interconnecting the subcultures resemble a plate of spaghetti flung across a slippery kitchen floor. Links emerge, shift, dissipate, re-form, go underground, erupt, waste away, and die. Both intersubculture and intrasubculture channels are dug, blocked, deepened, circumvented, dredged, and filled. More important, the human energy that flows along these ethereal canals often jumps channel and slices a new pathway to an adjoining conduit. Subcultures make strange bedfellows. Indeed, it seems somehow beyond comprehension that people ever thought that a management team could—at least, for long—guide such an organic system in a "scientific" manner. Ironically, some company cultures ordain that people not speak openly about the organization's culture. A culture of denial is still a culture. Some company cultures forbid use of the word *culture,* preferring instead presumably less offensive substitutes such as *work environment* or *organization climate.* A culture of obfuscation is still a culture.

Paradoxically, a culture both shapes what people think, feel, say, and do and is shaped by what people think, feel, say, and do. Culture is a self-reinforcing system. And . . . culture rules. Why is this? Life seems to be wired to culture. While we once thought that culture and learning were the sole domains of *Homo sapiens sapiens,* modern behavioral research suggests that animals great and small also have cultures, and testing demonstrates how culture is handed down from generation to generation in the animal kingdom. Can we humans be that different? We don't think so—because culture sets the ground rules for how the members of an organization *should* behave. And those who do not comply are reviled, mistreated, or cast out. An organization's culture thus has a saturating impact on its members. If the culture is grounded in trust, creativity, and mutual benefit, chances are the organization itself is prospering or in the process of adapting to get back on track. If the culture is closed, fearful, and based on win-lose outcomes, chances are it is in, or on the brink of, a death spiral.

Lee Dugatkin (2001), associate professor of biology at the University of Louisville, and Frans B. M. de Waal (2001), professor of primate behavior at Emory University in Atlanta, have reported on the growing body of evidence indicating that animals, like human beings, both learn from each other and pass that learning on to others. Sow black bears teach their cubs how to climb, hunt, and forage. Raccoons teach their kits how to wash food. Dolphins teach their calves how to gang up on sharks. The formal term to describe this dynamic is *cultural transmission*. If we use the definition of culture found in *Webster's New Collegiate Dictionary* (1974), "the integrated pattern of human behavior that includes thought, speech, action, and artifacts and depends upon man's capacity for learning and transmitting knowledge to succeeding generations" (5a), people also engage in cultural transmission. Anthropologists have long reported on how the practices of so-called primitive tribes persist long after the reasons for those customs have vanished into mythology. Druidic fertility celebrations survive as May Day merriments. Leather pouches filled with medicinal herbs show up to today in a wide array of "good luck" charms: a rabbit's foot tucked away in a pocket, a religious icon hung around the neck, or wind chimes hanging on the front porch. Ancient sacrifices and libations are reenacted every time a child tosses a penny into a wishing well. These practices serve as cultural symbols of good luck, success, and prosperity. Culturally, we are told that if we do these things, we will be safe, we will succeed. And these cultural messages are reinforced by the most powerful of motivations. We want to be accepted and loved within our culture, and we want to succeed. We see others engage in the activity and we want to do it, too.

Dugatkin tells the story of guppies and how they do what they see other guppies doing regardless of how they may be hard-wired to react. Habitually, it seems, female guppies tend to want to mate with bright orange male guppies. This preference is a genetic thing. In an experiment to see if female guppies would change their fondness for bright orange male guppies, Dugatkin arranged it so that female guppies could view both bright orange and dull-colored guppies at the same time. But with a trick using opaque and see-through dividers, the females saw what appeared to be other females selecting dull-colored guppies. What happened next surprised the researcher. Female guppies viewing other females selecting dull-colored males began to do the same, overriding their hard-wired instinct to mate with the bright orange males. This phenomenon is known as "date copying." It seems that among the mating rituals of American university students, if one popular and good-looking student dates a certain type of person, others want to date that type, too. Marketers have exploited variations of date copying for years by showing happy, good-looking people using their products, knowing that you, too, will want to use them. Be like a hero athlete by using the brand of deodorant she applies with a captivating smile.

In organization culture, anyone who has witnessed elaborate management rituals knows about cultural transmission. IBM is not known as "Big Blue" because of the color of its corporate logo or the boxes the computers are housed in. No, the name comes from the respectable color of the suit to be worn by IBM's managers as mandated by Thomas J. Watson, Sr., and continued by his son. Wear a blue suit and you will be loved, dated, and succeed. What formidable messages culture transmits. Culture can override instincts, intellect, and even values. The key implication, of course, is that if an organization's leaders see the value of rewiring their company with a partnering culture, then they themselves must initiate smart partnering behaviors. If you shout "red suit" but continue to wear blue suits, people will wear blue suits. Leaders not prepared to risk failure by trying smart partnering behaviors must be confronted promptly, given a choice and a chance, and then replaced if they continue to display divisive behaviors.

Bottom-Line Business Results Rooted in Culture

How executives, managers, and employees regard shareholders, how they treat customers, and how they esteem each other all echo cultural prescripts. How the members of an organization go about determining what kind of culture they need to accelerate company growth is itself a cultural gauntlet. The ability to recognize strengths and acknowledge weaknesses is a cultural issue. Some cultures rot, emaciated by the omnivorous microbes of denial, fear, dishonesty, and delusion. Other cultures prosper, invigorated by the irrepressible catalysts of creativity, risk taking, integrity, and self-evaluation. Most often, cultures are paradoxical systems containing both productive and counterproductive characteristics. Regardless of an organization's cultural traits, the ethereal energies they drive in the people who live and work within the structure will foretell their success or failure.

LEADERS AND THE ORIGINS OF AN ORGANIZATION CULTURE

Culture springs mainly from how leaders behave: what they say and do, and how they say and do it. Culture is forged and communicated in the messages they send about what is important and what is not important, what is acceptable and not acceptable, and who is valued and who is not valued. Most messages leaders send are nonverbal. Everyone watches and listens for clues to ascertain with assurance the boundaries of acceptable behavior to determine the zone within which they can safely operate. This safety zone solidifies the norms of behavior. The end result is culture, a direct result of the behavior of leaders.

An anthropological example will illustrate the power of a culture to shape the behavior of its members. Because the Maya worshiped the sun and the moon as gods, their priests—their "executive team"—instituted a taboo against making objects shaped like the sun or moon. Circles became a really big no-no. As a consequence, the Maya only rarely constructed circular structures (the astronomical observatory at Chichén Itzá is one example), and they never developed the wheel. No wheels meant no long-range transportation and no mechanical engines. No engines, no industry. Mayan clerics did, however, get fairly adept at cutting out the throbbing hearts of still-living sacrificial victims to honor their gods and assure a bountiful harvest. The winners of the Mayan court ball game (played something like modern-day soccer), according to some sources, earned the right to slay the losers and run victory laps while hoisting the oozing heads of the now decapitated losers in one hand and a mug of home-brew in the other. Win or get whacked. Talk about performance management! Much to the delight of the drunken upper-class spectators, these games sometimes went on for weeks and were said to be "spirited." Really. Culture does drop to the bottom line.

How many good ideas, products, and services are waiting in closets because the behaviors of an organization's leaders inhibit or squash risk taking? The ability to take a risk or not is just one gauge of an organization culture. Assume, for example, that you belong to a closed, fear-based organization. You believe the company needs to take a risk in the marketplace with a breakthrough technology, product, or service. However, because anxiety fixates the firm, its leaders refuse to take the risk. They bicker, they deny, they delay. Then they ask for more data. This executive dithering precludes the opportunity to secure the resources needed to bring your new offering to market, along with the potential of revitalizing the business. The company languishes under the weight of fear and timidity. The opportunity passes or, worse, a competitor snatches it.

On the other hand, some business cultures thrive on risk. Nokia, a manufacturer of wireless telecommunications equipment, knew that its customers were increasingly younger and younger. It therefore decided to break the color barrier of wireless handsets. Until then, you could get a handset in any color, as long as it was black. Nokia started to produce handsets in all sorts of colors, with a rainbow of appliqués, and soon became the number one manufacturer of wireless handsets. Was their technology any better? No. Their leaders set up an environment in which an individual felt comfortable taking a risk.

Innovation can intimidate because of traits embedded in the psyche of the people who live in a risk-averse culture—in this case, fear. Fear, a powerful negative energy, drives predictably defensive behaviors within an organization. In the example of the fear-based organization above, leaders punished risk takers. And the legacy and the residue of that negative energy continue to haunt that company to this day. Once the wagons are circled, it takes extraordinary leadership and a big kick in the backside to get them back on the trail.

Culture by Evolution or by Design?

Culture plays such a vital role in the success of an organization that leaders can no longer afford to leave it to chance. Yet, as crucial as culture is to bottom-line results, most leaders spend little time reflecting on the constructs or consequences of their cultures. Leaders do from time to time prattle on about culture (or appropriate euphemisms). They publicly espouse the implications of it for their business, employees, and customers. Yet they personally continue to behave in the same ways and are puzzled that their subordinates are not changing. Culture is something to throw change management programs at. It's one of those people things for the human resources department to worry about. Forging culture, it seems, is not part of an executive's *real* job!

Cultures materialize in two principal ways. The most common method, "culture by evolution," happens when no deliberate thought or design is applied to the configuration of an organization's culture. With few exceptions, most corporate cultures have evolved in this manner, especially many of the brick-and-mortar industries that are the stalwarts of Wall Street today. Rarely did their founders have insight on the importance of molding a specific culture to help them succeed in their marketplace. More important, seldom were they aware that what they were doing and saying and how they were doing and saying it would fashion their company's culture. What Bill Procter and Jim Gamble started at the suggestion of their father-in-law over 150 years ago still molds both the strategic and tactical decisions being made at Procter & Gamble headquarters in Cincinnati. For all the brothers-in-law knew, they were just manufacturing and selling candles (Procter) and soap (Gamble). They were less interested that they were inventing brand management. But they were.

Culture by design happens when leaders sit down and formulate a culture and then rigorously communicate and live by its tenets. Few businesses have consciously taken this more purposeful path, though some have had the advantage of having leaders with an unconscious competency in the area. On the other hand, many religious and nonprofit organizations were founded around a tightly knit set of ideals and are recharged daily by these principles. For example, Benedictine monks still live by the simple precept of hospitality to strangers and the maxim *Ora et Labora* (pray and work), though St. Benedict set these norms over fifteen hundred years ago. Member physicians and nurses of Doctors Without Borders, often at the peril of their lives, abide by the principle of treating the needy regardless of nationality, ethnic origin, or social class. If we asked how the International Red Cross and the International Red Crescent serve their communities, almost anyone would be able to come up with examples. The pertinent lesson of these nonprofit organizations is that cultures that have been designed to champion a powerful purpose stand the test of time. Religious faith has kept people—often separated by vast distances in space and time—connected with each other long before the World-Wide Web, or e-mail, or instant messaging. The most deep-seated ties that bind are ethereal, not material.

In the twenty-first century, a business that wants to stay alive, and thrive, must learn the lessons of a designed culture. Pick one and learn from it. Better yet, take a week and go live in a monastic community. For with a culture by design, leaders must think resolutely about the atmosphere, environment, and customs that they want to permeate their organization. In their gut, they must make the connection between their organization's purpose and the culture required to sustain that purpose. Moreover, they must take stock of their own ability and willingness to model the attitudes and behaviors they are seeking and realistically assess if they are truly acting as they want others to act.

The scandals in corporate accounting and the trading shenanigans in the fund industry have prompted some organizations to refocus on the role of culture in influencing the behavior of employees. As this book was going to press, Morningstar, a firm that rates the performance of mutual funds, announced that it was going to begin rating mutual funds on five governance issues. One of these issues for which each fund will be assigned a letter grade from A to F is corporate culture. Yes, investors, you will soon be able to see in the clear light of day whether or not a particular fund with which you have entrusted your bucks has failed corporate culture. What fund manager wants to bring home that report card?

LEADING BY EXAMPLE

Leading by example is perhaps the biggest challenge that confronts business leaders today. It is personally risky. While many leaders can mouth the platitudes of cultural attributes, they cannot hide how they act. Talking about "walking the talk" is much easier than actually walking the talk. We have a colleague who says he is going to title his next book *This Stuff Is a Whole Lot Harder to Do Than It Looks!* How leaders act reverberates profoundly throughout an organization. Throw a pebble into a tranquil pond and watch the ripples move out over the water, eventually reaching the outer shores. It is amazing how this one little intrusive act on the serene surface sets a whole body of water into motion. And, not just once—when the ripples reach the outer shores, they reverse themselves and start to move back toward the epicenter.

Much like the pebble disturbing the surface of the pond, contradictory leadership behaviors stir movement in ways that unsettle the organization from one end to the other, and then unsettle it again and again as the ripples bounce around in all directions. When a leader's personal actions undercut his or her public words, the discord it creates in the organization reverberates in ways that are difficult to predict.

The CEO of a company says he wants to establish a culture of openness and trust. He talks about it whenever he brings his executive team together. He believes he believes it. He believes he is passionate about it. But when sales begin to fall, he summons the vice president of marketing and sales to his office and berates her, warning her that she is not doing enough. "I don't want to hear excuses, just get those damn sales up! I don't care what you have to do!" A ripple in the pond has begun to spread out in every direction. She does her best to shield her team members from the abuse she has taken. She does not share with her people the details of her conversation with the CEO. She reports to them that the meeting was "OK," but somehow the nonverbal, unconscious signals are being relayed to her team with every breath she takes. In response to being dressed down, she changes her day-to-day behaviors—without realizing it. She thinks she is continuing to behave with executive deportment. But before long, people sense that something is wrong. The level of anxiety rises. All across the pond the water becomes more and more agitated, murky, unpredictable.

Suddenly, all the flowery talk of openness and trust vanishes as people hunker down and do what they need to do to protect themselves. Fear *will* motivate action. But the movement will be without soul, without creativity, and without passion as folks recoil into a state of compliance. Spending valuable energy on protecting themselves, they have less *oomph* available for thinking of the creative, new strategies needed to meet sales quotas. Groups acting out of fear may accomplish a short-term objective, but the organization pays a high price in other ways. Cultures that run on fear typically have high turnover rates, low retention, excessive recruiting and staffing costs, and a high degree of burnout among executives and employees alike. That's the cost of "poor culture."

Critics, for example, have pointed out that GE, often lauded as one of the best-managed companies in the world, has this anxiety syndrome. Based on certain financial indicators, GE looks great on paper. But, say critics, the dark side is the culture of stress and fear that dictates that unless you are number one, or getting there fast, you will be replaced. An in-depth analysis of the organization would show that much of its growth has been accomplished by acquisition and that many of its core products are in fact not market leaders in quality, design, or desirability. The appliance division, for example, is a fast follower at best. By using a strategy of bulk purchasing and subsidizing customers in the form of low-interest rates using GE Financial Services prowess, GE is able to force product into new housing units and mass-market retailers with the slimmest of margins. Yet, when consumers upgrade their major appliances, they look to Sweden's Asko, Germany's Bosch, or America's Sub-Zero for high-end design and quality. GE will copy what you see on these high-end manufacturers' showroom floors—a couple years later. In due course, inability to think creatively, take risks, and move beyond the boundaries set by the cultural straitjacket will stifle their potential. Without a profound cultural shift, the existing win-or-go-home, fear-driven rubrics will eventually sap the organization of the creative energy it needs to continue to succeed in the marketplace. Remember when you could be sure if it's Westinghouse?

2

Building a Partnering Organization

Those who have given out of their stock to any particular city without requiring any return from it receive what they lack from another to which they have given nothing. Thus, the whole island is like a single family.

—THOMAS MORE, *UTOPIA*

Given how vital organization culture is to the success of an enterprise, a company's leaders sooner or later will face this question: Is our current culture going to get us where we want to go? This question should be keeping business leaders up at night. For if the answer is "no" or "not likely" or "maybe," another question arises: What kind of culture will get us where we want to go? And then a third: How do we get there from here? This implies three more pointed questions:

- How are legacy subcultures driving current behaviors, both productive and counterproductive?

- What is the fastest, cheapest way to introduce a new culture?

- How do we make the new culture stick?

Inasmuch as undertaking to change an organization's culture is one of the most difficult and costly endeavors on which a leadership team can embark, leaders must confidently know the answers to these key questions.

A PARTNERING ORGANIZATION

If you conclude that your current organization is not going to get you where you want to go, we suggest that a partnering organization will. Table 1 illustrates examples of behavioral differences between a traditional organization and a partnering organization. By *traditional organization* we mean an enterprise governed principally according to a hierarchical, postindustrial—predominantly military—management model: command and control.

TABLE 1
Characteristics of a Partnering Organization

TRADITIONAL ORGANIZATION	PARTNERING ORGANIZATION
Keeps information close to the vest and dodges chances to give colleagues feedback *"Silence is golden."*	Self-discloses information freely and gives feedback straightforwardly *"Give it to me straight"*
Solves problems based on self-interest and wins by creating losers *"Winning is everything."*	Solves problems creatively and resolves conflicts collaboratively, creating winners, not losers *"We both benefit from this."*
Expresses and demonstrates low trust in others *"Trust but verify."*	Builds trust through both words and actions *"I know you'll do the right thing"*
Relies mainly on past history in making decisions *"Let's get back to basics."*	Embraces the future with a clear vision *"The future belongs to us"*
Clings to status quo and fights change *"The more things change, the more they stay the same."*	Encourages, welcomes, and leverages change *"This way is so much better!"*
Promotes self-reliance: *"I'd rather do it myself."*	Champions interreliance with others for key results: *"Can you believe what we accomplished together?"*

The "Traditional Organization" column in Table 1 includes clichés emphasizing how values contrary to partnering exist in many current business communities. Language shapes how we look at things, and how we look at things influences our behaviors. Leaders thus must avoid such clichés and begin to link the commonsense language of partnering with consistent behavior that reinforces their words to achieve the desired results. Behaviors such as those included in Table 1 are not in and of themselves necessarily good or bad, valuable or worthless, productive or counterproductive. The same behavior that produces desired results in one kind of organization might trigger catastrophe in another. Colonel Gregory "Pappy" Boyington, a World War II marine fighter pilot with twenty-eight shootdowns, recaps what distinguishes an ace from an average fighter pilot in *Baa Baa Black Sheep* (1977):

> *There is just a split second where everything is right, for the target is going to remain anything but stationary. During this split second the range has to be just right, the deflection has to be accurate, and the first squeeze of the trigger has to be as smooth and perfect as humanly possible. In other words months of preparation, one of those few opportunities, and the judgment of a split second are what makes some pilot an ace, while others think back on what they could have done.* (141)

Compare Colonel Boyington's appraisal of the importance of decisiveness for a fighter pilot with that of M. R. D. Foot in describing the recruitment of British secret agents in *SOE: An Outline History of the Special Operations Executive, 1940–1946* (1999):

> *There was one character trait in particular that he found he had to watch out for, and avoid: impulsiveness. Prudence, after courage, was probably an agent's most useful quality. Brisk, decisive types, inclined to make up their minds promptly, were all very well in fast traffic or a destroyer action, but were not what was needed in the secret war. There the need was for reflective men and women, people who could look several moves ahead.* (72)

The behaviors that enable aces to shoot down enemy planes would get secret agents killed. The behaviors that enable secret agents to cause disarray behind enemy lines would get fighter pilots killed. Same behaviors, dissimilar situations, the difference between success and failure.

Traditional organizations in large part adopt systems, processes, and rules intended to safeguard the enterprise's assets and minimize risks. In the marketplace, they usually operate more defensively than offensively. Not making mistakes is more highly valued than "going for it." Avoiding risk is a more dominant business driver than is seeking opportunities. Let's hold on to what we have. Thus, traditional organizations as a rule constrain accountability (through authorization tables), divide labor (through detailed job descriptions), compartmentalize functions (by physically insulating departments and people from each other), and control accomplishment of tasks (through multiple layers of management and narrow spans of control).

A traditional organization invests enormous resources in watchers: watchers to watch watchers who are watching watchers watching people who are actually doing work—inventing products and services, making and delivering products and services, marketing and selling products and services. The simplistic presumption is that more watchers equals less risk. Members of a traditional organization are recognized and rewarded for displaying behaviors that reinforce these protective systems. People might get mad if they knew what salary their colleagues really make, so payroll information is kept tightly under wraps; employees traveling on company business might abuse their expense accounts, so their meal expenses are capped at $50 a day; promotions are touted as "competitive," so employees sense that they might be undercutting their own advancement opportunities if they pitch in to help a colleague who has found himself in a pinch. Many of these behaviors stem from a view of organizations as being a "zero-sum game": for me to win, someone else must lose.

In a partnering organization, behavior is not driven by such a scarcity mentality, but rather by an abundance mentality. If we partner, we get our personal, professional, and organizational needs met—at levels not possible in a competitive environment, not to mention organization cultures that actively encourage cutthroat behavior among their leaders and employees. A partnering organization tends to attack the marketplace more offensively than will a traditional organization, seeing changes—whether economic, social, political, financial, or otherwise—primarily as opportunities for growth and expansion, rather than as threats. Not that a partnering organization chucks internal financial controls overboard or does not conduct ongoing analyses of business risks. However, once the leaders of a partnering organization have weighed both the opportunities and the risks, they are much more likely to "go for it" than their more risk-averse counterparts in a traditional organization.

In a partnering organization, the catchphrase "together we can get more for everybody" guides behavior more often than the "let's hold on to what we've got" mantra repeated in traditional organizations. Thus, partnering organizations give people a broad range of accountabilities (through strategic directives), connect people (through partnering charters), unify functions (by physically positioning departments and people close to each other), and delegate accomplishment of tasks (through fewer layers of management and broad spans of control). A partnering organization invests enormous resources in finding, keeping, and developing smart partners: doers—not watchers—who appreciate the potency of partnering and who take personal accountability for delivering on commitments by collaborating, internally and externally, with whomever it makes sense to do so. The members of a partnering organization are recognized and rewarded for displaying the partnering behaviors that deliver results for everyone involved. Partnering organizations replace the zero-sum game rule book with guidelines anchored by a "we all win" outlook. Smart partners win not only because of what they do, but also because of how they do it.

PARTNERING ORGANIZATIONS NEED A PARTNERING CULTURE

How do they get one? To build a partnering organization that will last longer than a few vision rollout pitches, leaders must create a partnering culture. A partnering culture's purpose is not primarily to eradicate existing subcultures. In fact, a partnering culture both leverages the strengths of legacy subcultures and tames their counterproductive behaviors by replacing them with the productive behaviors of smart partnering. A partnering culture is a governing culture that reduces the risk of the culture wars that typically break out when company leaders decide to drive "new culture" into an organization. A partnering culture aims first at expediting internal alliances among an organization's diverse functions and second at extending the same partnering expertise externally to forge mutually beneficial relationships with other companies.

Given the level of impact that leadership behaviors have on forming and sustaining any organization culture, as discussed in Chapter 1, leaders who want to create a partnering culture must be willing to modify their own behaviors and invest resources in installing the infrastructure and processes required for building the organization's partnering quotient, or PQ. Since it is not businesses that partner, but rather people who partner, this approach to organization culture change implies that each person in the enterprise— beginning with the leadership team—works in a systematic way to understand and develop his or her individual PQ. A practical means of helping people understand their partnering strengths and weaknesses is Stephen Dent's Partnering Quotient Assessment™ (the PQ Assessment™), a self-assessment of the Six Partnering Attributes: Self-Disclosure and Feedback, Win-Win Orientation, Ability to Trust, Future Orientation, Comfort with Change, and Comfort with Interdependence.* Table 2 summarizes how these six attributes of Partnering Intelligence are linked to the behavioral characteristics of a partnering organization listed in Table 1.

Remember, in that a partnering culture is a governing culture, its highest value is combining the greatest strengths of each of its subcultures. A partnering culture fosters collaboration among existing subcultures, rather than cutthroat competition. Rewiring an organization for a partnering culture does not mandate the rooting out and extermination of various legacy subcultures. Rather, it taps and catalyzes the energy of the divergent subcultures. We do want R&D explorers to stare off into space, imagining new product and service offerings; we do need engineers to fret about the seventh decimal place in an equation for calculating sheer; we do require a marketing and sales team that chomps at the bit to sell more widgets; and we must have enablers such as financial analysts, information technologists, and human resources professionals to serve as organizational glue.

---

*For more detailed information on the Six Partnering Attributes, see Stephen M. Dent, *Partnering Intelligence,* 2d ed. (Palo Alto, CA: Davies-Black Publishing, 2004).

TABLE 2
Attributes of a Partnering Organization

PARTNERING ORGANIZATION	PARTNERING ATTRIBUTE
Self-discloses information freely and gives feedback straightforwardly	**Self-Disclosure and Feedback**
Solves problems creatively and resolves conflicts collaboratively, creating winners, not losers	**Win-Win Orientation**
Builds trust through both words and actions	**Ability to Trust**
Embraces the future with a clear vision	**Future Orientation**
Encourages and welcomes change	**Comfort with Change**
Champions interreliance with others for key results	**Comfort with Interdependence**

Because of the systematic nature of the Six Partnering Attributes, each of the characteristics contributes to a complex web of interactions between people. For simplicity, we have made explicit connections in Table 2 only to the dominant links. For example, Self-Disclosure and Feedback and Future Orientation constitute overriding links among the six characteristics of a partnering organization because envisioning an inspiring future depends on both letting go of the past and exchanging information freely and collaboratively. Thus, although Self-Disclosure and Feedback and Future Orientation play primary roles, the other four attributes also contribute to the success of an inspired vision. Following is an overview of each of the Six Partnering Attributes.

Self-Disclosure and Feedback

Unless our partners are like the Vulcans on *Star Trek,* proficient in the telepathic art of "mind melding," the only way for our partners to know what we need or want is by our telling them. Self-disclosure represents the initial opportunity to form trust in a relationship. The more information you reveal to your partners about yourself, the more your partners will trust you, and the more readily they will open up to you. Self-disclosure sets the stage for giving and receiving feedback, crucial to airing and resolving conflicts. If you cannot safely provide feedback to partners on their behavior, you must suppress your opinions and feelings. Such restraint invariably leads to resentment, a breakdown in communication, and counterproductive behaviors. The partnering culture attribute Self-Disclosure and Feedback enables each of the diverse subcultures of a company to get its needs met, the fundamental purpose of partnering. Moreover, in successful partnerships, self-disclosure and feedback are conscious acts. Disclosing our wants and needs, thoughts and feelings, strengths and weaknesses is essential if all parties are to achieve their goals and obtain mutual benefits.

Win-Win Orientation

Creating win-win outcomes goes to the heart of a partnering culture. Acting in a win-win manner means that you use problem-solving and conflict resolution strategies that benefit all parties involved. Remember, partnerships are formed to fulfill needs. The two primary desired outcomes of a win-win orientation are therefore getting your needs met and getting your partner's needs met. How each of us gets these needs met forms a vital ingredient in the system that creates productive and successful partnerships. Solving task-related problems involves the same kinds of approaches required to resolve interpersonal conflicts. Regardless of the nature of the problem, task or relationship, you want to resolve it in a way that meets your needs. When others are also at the table, they too will want to ensure that their needs are met. If the two sets of needs initially seem to be incompatible, the partnering culture attribute Win-Win Orientation is essential. We are not born with the negotiating skills needed to

achieve outcomes that are mutually beneficial; we must learn them
and get better and better at them.

Ability to Trust

In interacting with others, our safety and well-being depend on our
ability to interpret correctly a complex, shifting system of symbols
and signals. As we grow, we discover with whom we are safe and with
whom we are in danger. We learn what we can do and what kinds of
reactions we can provoke in others. This system of reliable responses
binds together our social order. We call it trust. When we violate
established norms and expectations, we confuse and upset others.
Such a rupture in these ground rules is typically sensed as a violation
of trust. In business, establishing and maintaining trust is often difficult. A competitive culture rewards enterprises that act in new and
unpredictable ways, often with little regard for the comfort of its people, its customers, or its competitors. The partnering culture attribute Ability to Trust forms the foundation of a work climate in which
people know and appreciate the limits of reliability and can be sure
that these borders will be respected. Trust is the one characteristic of
a partnering culture that is at once both an input into the partnership
and an output of the partnership. Trust encourages harmony and
generosity. A lack of trust sometimes leads to people acting in angry,
hostile, or other counterproductive ways. The people in an organization build trust when they consistently satisfy each other's expectations.
Only one experience of betrayal will threaten even the best-crafted
partnership.

Future Orientation

Having a past or future orientation sets the overall tone for a relationship, the background music of personal interactions, whether harmo-
nious or harsh. Since partnerships are organic in nature, it can determine
in large part whether or not the relationship will succeed. Our orientation toward the past or toward the future determines many aspects of
a partnership before we even sit down to work with our partners. It
determines how flexible and trusting we are likely to be and, in particular, how much risk we are willing to take. If the leaders of an

organization have a past orientation, the business typically runs as a closed system. People in such a company have difficulty with change and fight to maintain the status quo. Decisions come from the top down, and there is little genuine communication between managers and workers. Functional groups behave as fiefdoms. Managers battle for resources. It is all a zero-sum game. Smart partners, on the contrary, know themselves well enough to keep from getting trapped in the past, and they trust themselves to make new plans and try innovative approaches. Like trust, the partnering culture attribute Future Orientation serves as a kind of lubricant for the organization. If a business has a past orientation, it tends to impose past experience on new situations. If it has a future orientation, it is more likely to see the possibilities in new situations and approach them with hope and good faith. A future orientation shouts, "Go for it!"

Comfort with Change

Over 2,500 years ago the Greek philosopher Heraclitus noted that nothing is permanent except change. Accelerating social and technological changes continue to barrage us. We change computers, cars, and jobs with ever-increasing speed. Organizations respond to this continual change in various ways: some strive to minimize change, while others enthusiastically embrace it, even create it. In any event, change happens. The key to coping with changing relationships and a changing business landscape is to remember that although we may not always be able to control change, we can manage how we respond to it, productively or counterproductively. Because enterprises today are drenched with changes, the partnering culture attribute Comfort with Change enables an organization to identify obstacles to change, develop strategies for coping with them, and formulate action plans for implementing desired business changes. In the broadest sense, the perceived need to do something differently drives the formation of partnerships. Just like individuals, organizations need change and renewal. Survival, reinvigoration, or growth determines why an organization might risk reaching out to form a partnership or strategic alliance. Each business partner wants something it cannot get, or get easily, on its own. This act of reaching out, of being willing to do something differently, in and of itself will disrupt the status quo and precipitate change.

Comfort with Interdependence

In Western cultures we do not use the word *interdependence* much. We champion individuals and we have built societies and explored the globe by hard work and independence. We value making it on our own—"I'd rather do it myself"—and we "look out for number one." Other cultures value independence to a lesser degree. People share resources and rely on one another to get their mutual needs met. What benefits the group benefits its individuals, and vice versa. This mutuality forms the essence of interdependence. The marketplaces of the twentieth century thrived on independence and competition. Today, however, with exploding technologies and growing demand for complex goods and services, businesses are finding that they cannot satisfy all their operating needs. The partnering culture attribute Comfort with Interdependence encourages enterprises both to do business differently inside and to look outside for new kinds of strategic partners. When leaders value interdependence, they create an environment that encourages involvement. With that participation comes a sense that we're all in this together, and information and other resources flow freely. Our comfort with interdependence thus serves as the heart of the marketplace component of organization culture. These collaborative strategies require us to create partnerships in which all sides profit from our mutual success. Achieving interdependence does not happen by a top-floor fiat to partner. Interdependence is an active, ongoing process that requires all parties to move apace from initial independence to vibrant collaboration.

LEADING BY EXAMPLE IN A PARTNERING ORGANIZATION

Chapter 1 stressed how the behaviors of leaders serve as major forces in creating an organization's culture, whether accidentally forming a *culture by evolution* or purposefully shaping a *culture by design*. For leaders who want to create a partnering culture, the first step is to figure out how they have to change their personal behavior. How should a partnering leader act? What must he or she do more of? Less of? Start doing? Stop doing? Do in different ways? Do here but not there? There but not here? Table 3, an extension of Table 2, gives

TABLE 3
Leader's Role in a Partnering Organization

PARTNERING ORGANIZATION	PARTNERING ATTRIBUTE	LEADER'S ROLE
Self-discloses information freely and gives feedback straightforwardly	Self-Disclosure and Feedback	■ Establish a safe atmosphere for open communication ■ Monitor personal reaction to information ■ Reward candidness and diversity of thought ■ Seek feedback ■ "Walk the corridors"
Solves problems creatively and resolves conflicts collaboratively, creating winners, not losers	Win-Win Orientation	■ Build agreements on how conflict will be resolved ■ Be aware of and monitor personal reaction to conflict ■ Create awareness of conflict styles ■ Make a conscious effort to move to a win-win negotiator style
Builds trust through both words and actions	Ability to Trust	■ Define trust within organization ■ Define behaviors associated with building and diminishing trust at both a relationship and task level ■ Monitor and be aware of personal trust style ■ Establish trust as an organizational measurement ■ Reward trust-building behaviors
Embraces the future with a clear vision	Future Orientation	■ Define expectations for future orientation ■ Monitor personal language and behavior based on future orientation ■ Educate people about future orientation ■ Hold people accountable for future-oriented decision making ■ Recognize and reward innovation based on future orientation

representative examples of the kinds of partnering behaviors that leaders must display consistently if they truly wish to create a partnering culture.

TABLE 3 CONTINUED
Leader's Role in a Partnering Organization

PARTNERING ORGANIZATION	PARTNERING ATTRIBUTE	LEADER'S ROLE
Encourages and welcomes change	Comfort with Change	• Understand personal change style • Recognize benefits and stressors to change • Acknowledge others' change style and plan for a range of reactions • Allow others to control the impacts of change that fall within their scope of responsibility • Reward change behaviors • Monitor change events to prevent "change overload"
Champions interreliance with others for key results	Comfort with Interdependence	• Acknowledge to direct reports your dependence on them for your success • Align reward structure to compensate for partnering behaviors • Align organizational priorities • Link cross-functional results to organizational objectives • Rotate job responsibilities at the managerial level • Establish formal partnership agreements between executives and departments

BENEFITS OF A PARTNERING CULTURE

Creating a partnering culture positions an organization to accrue four chief benefits:

- **Openness**—being sensitive to shifts in attitudes and trends

- **Creativity**—inventing and innovating new products and services

- **Agility**—responding quickly to both opportunities and threats

- **Resiliency**—hanging in there and bouncing back

What can these four benefits mean to an organization? Let's look at each of them now briefly (they are described in fuller detail in Chapters 8–10 and the conclusion, respectively).

Openness

A partnering culture encourages the smart partnering attribute Self-Disclosure and Feedback. Without accurate information about a trading partner's needs and wants, the success of any marketplace exchange falls largely to chance. More often than not, someone does not get what she wanted and resentment, recrimination, and retaliation may soon follow—overtly in some instances but more commonly covertly. In a company in which people value and practice the art of self-disclosure and feedback, higher levels of openness become easier to attain.

Openness is more than passive receptivity to communication. Rather, our definition of the word encompasses the broader meaning of being in tune with both the stimulants and the depressants in an environment, recognizing both the elixirs and the poisons. For example, what are your customers saying to their friends and neighbors about the last time they called your customer care center and were put on hold for a half-hour? Seeing a market segment accurately and fully is made easier and quicker when many, rather than fewer, eyeballs are scanning the landscape. A partnering infrastructure enables the systematic syncing up of the binoculars of all the partners. Everyone sees more, everyone benefits. Smart partnering produces enhanced openness. Smart partnering helps you see the marketplace.

Creativity

In a partnering culture, creativity comes about most directly from two partnering attributes: Future Orientation and Comfort with Change. Together they form a sturdy platform for creativity and innovation. Creativity at its heart involves seeing the same old things in new ways, letting go of how one has viewed things and done things in the past. Leaders locked primarily in a past orientation—shackled by predispositions about what *should* be there, certain that the way it was is the way it is—will find it hard to encourage working men and women to strike out in new directions. A partnering culture, on the other hand, establishes future orientation as a basic tenet. Yet, having a future orientation without being comfortable with change will produce only empty dreams, illusory aspirations, and delusional desires.

Comfort with Change steadies us to take the plunge, to risk belittlement, punishment, even failure.

Agility

In the twenty-first century, agility, the best risk-management tool any enterprise can have, will require more than nimbleness and speed of foot. Agility now requires competence and resources. The trick, of course, is bringing together competent people with the resources they need in a quick, efficient manner. Going forward, fewer and fewer companies will have the bucks or the bravado to house all the competencies they need or to warehouse all the resources they need. Without the expediting function of a partnering infrastructure, organizations will find it increasingly difficult to act with the agility required to leverage budding opportunities or to defend against impending threats.

In a partnering culture, the smart partnering attribute Win-Win Orientation forms the currency of marketplaces. Interconnections among marketplaces give an organization ready access to competencies and resources it does not possess in-house. Links build agility. Outsourcing and cosourcing are the more formal kinds of relationships that can be consummated in this regard. However, advantage in the twenty-first century will more likely derive from the *informal links* among marketplaces . . . talking across backyard fences. Bolstered by the smart partnering attribute Ability to Trust, an element that must support win-win solutions to assure ongoing agility, informal exchanges across marketplaces will deliver competent people, information, technology, and material to where it is needed, when it is needed, how it is needed, at the price desired. Free-flowing talent and resources will redefine the kind of agility an organization will require to survive and thrive. Smart partnering creates the connections, dredges the channels deep, and propels the traffic.

Resiliency

When all six attributes of a partnering culture work together to reinforce each other, a partnering organization achieves resiliency. To sustain itself, to adjust continually to changes beyond its control, to see what others do not, and to capitalize on those insights, an organization must be instilled thoroughly with all six attributes of smart partnering, but especially with Comfort with Interdependence. Exponentially accelerating performance will result when partnering is "how things are done around here" and we trust each other to partner smartly. What Comfort with Interdependence adds to the mix is the sustainability that results when I am willing to carry some of your load and you are willing to carry some of mine. And neither of us complains about having to do someone else's job.

Comfort with Interdependence in particular enables continuity and vibrancy in marketplaces. The great leap forward occurs when I finally trust you to help me get what I need after I have found out, usually the hard way, that I cannot get it for myself. To do this, I must let go of myself. French author Simone de Beauvoir once tendered in a *Life* magazine article in the late 1960s: "Freedom means only that I get to choose whose slave I will be." Liberated from the tyranny of self-reliance, I can now help you get what you need by accessing my network. A marketplace of one is by definition a self-abusive fantasy. Marketplaces want to be self-reinforcing, and it is in such self-reinforcement that an organization finds its resiliency. A summary of how all six characteristics of a partnering organization work together to produce resiliency, to create a Partnering Powerhouse, is provided in the conclusion.

I PARTNER, THEREFORE I AM . . . MORE

Organizations are struggling to react quickly to ever-changing customer needs, alliances among competitors, brand-new technologies, and top-talent wants and whims. Companies are straining to shift with market winds and financial swings, striving to outmaneuver and outlast competitors. Finding balance between the tasks and the relationships within and between organizations is key. Businesses are becoming organic networks, neural webs. A partnering culture appreciates the power of organic networks and embraces connectivity as the way we need to do our business every day. As our nomadic forebears did millennia ago, we will survive and grow only by making connections among one another, to the world around us, and to forces beyond our comprehension.

If you truly believe that things cannot be different, then they will stay the same. Too often we sink ourselves in the quicksand of fatalistic clichés such as "There's nothing new under the sun." Let's see, did physicians a thousand years ago know how the atrioventricular node routes bioelectric impulses along the pathways of a beating heart? Did astronomers one hundred years ago scan the sky with a radio telescope and see the Black Hole at the center of our galaxy? Did mathematicians ten years ago crank equations with a 2-GHz microprocessor? Creativity is at once both an act of faith and an act of hope. Ponder the insight of Fr. Pierre Teilhard de Chardin, writing in *Christianity and Evolution* (1964): "Nothing can any longer find place in our constructions which does not first satisfy the conditions of a *universe in process of transformation*" (78, emphasis added). I create, therefore I am.

In the world of commerce and industry, connectivity happens when enterprises form strategic alliances and partnerships within and among themselves. Creating a partnering culture requires hard work because most of us are, unknowingly, suspicious captives of a worldview that espouses disconnections and self-reliance as the quickest ways to success. I did it my way. My way or the highway. Successful leaders must understand and appreciate the profound marketplace implications of the human journey from connections to disconnections to reconnections. Zero sum must give way to infinite sum. New partnering cultures will thus need bracing but pliant transitional structures to enable connectivity values to take hold in the current hostile environment of disconnections. Alliances produce extraordinary results only when information flows freely and people trust each other and are loyal to one another. I partner, therefore I am . . . *more*.

To help leaders of an enterprise better understand how the existing organization culture is aligned or misaligned with the behavioral characteristics of a partnering organization, the authors employ a proprietary assessment instrument known as the Partnering Culture Survey. The survey data are presented to the company's leaders in the form of a six-dimensional Partnering Culture Profile, along with a specific set of staged, actionable recommendations for creating a Powerhouse Partner. In Chapter 3, we will begin sharing generic strategies and tactics for building a partnering organization, steps we have summarized in what we call the Powerhouse Partner Model.

3

Shaping Your Culture with the Powerhouse Partner Model

Few there are that rightly understand of what great advantage it is to blush at nothing and attempt everything.

—ERASMUS, *THE PRAISE OF FOLLY*

Imagine a government transportation agency spun off as a for-profit enterprise. It has conducted extensive research in the area of transportation. It has tested everything from the type of paint used to stripe lanes on highways to chemicals that melt snow and ice on mountain passes. It is a company of engineers housed in a campus-like setting in which each person has his or her own office with a window and a door that mostly stays shut. Suddenly, its leaders realize that the enterprise cannot continue to operate as an exclusive pool of independent, highly educated, well-paid individuals; rather, it has to operate as a collective to address and resolve transportation problems for clients around the world. Everyone needs to interact with each other to find the best solution for clients, and often that solution means combining talents and intelligences. The solution chosen was to construct a new building with an open-space office plan and move the engineers from offices with doors to open cubes with low walls to facilitate discussion, interaction, and teamwork.

What was this organization thinking? Only in hindsight did the leaders consider that employees might need help in adapting to this new environment and that adapting might require relationship and partnering skills. The example is one approach to building a new culture, though housing people in a new building with a new office layout is not going to change fundamentally how people interact and work together. Physical proximity is an important enabler—distance is a relentless adversary—but the ways in which people communicate and work together day in and day out are human activities that occur regardless of building design or office layout. The planners deserved credit for the ambitious open-plan design—after all, moving people from behind closed doors is a good beginning—but they failed to recognize the fundamentally human component of culture. Culture is not about the floorplan of a building. It's about how you lead people. It's about being aligned strategically and tactically, creating an enabling organization structure, hiring the right people, and offering incentives that recognize and reward the collaborative behaviors that create a partnering culture. Organizations do not partner; people partner.

THE POWER OF ORGANIZATION CULTURE

Among the greatest tragedies to hit the American space program have been the crashes of the space shuttles Challenger and Columbia. In the "Columbia Accident Investigation Board Report" (August 2003), the investigation board headed by Chairman Harold W. Gehman, Jr., Admiral, U.S. Navy (retired), concludes that the doomed flight of Columbia was attributed as much to "organizational failure" as technical failure. In the executive summary, the investigation board states:

> Cultural traits and organizational practices detrimental to safety were allowed to develop, including: reliance on past success as a substitute for sound engineering practices . . . organizational barriers that prevented effective communications of critical safety information and stifled professional differences of opinion; lack of integrated management across program elements; and the evolution of an informal chain of command and decision-making processes that operated outside the organization's rules. (vol. 1, p. 9)

While many will argue that organization culture has only a minimal impact on business, this investigation board has clearly identified culture as one of the major two areas of breakdown at NASA. Culture does drop to the bottom line.

In today's interconnected environment, task achievement alone will not propel an organization—or its stock valuation—to where its stakeholders demand that it go. In the Dual Age of Information and Connections, creating the value and innovation needed to move a company to the next level requires a focused effort on harnessing and releasing human potential and creativity. In most organizations, the worse things get operationally or financially, the more people tend to hunker down and do things. Ready, fire, aim. Or, fire, fire, fire. The mantra "better, faster, cheaper" can move organizations only so far. Then stuff starts to break.

Smart business people know that the route to "better, faster, cheaper" is, ironically, slower. Building relationships, communicating needs, and doing it right the first time result in less rework and higher-quality output, faster and cheaper. The only way to work smarter, not harder, in today's overloaded mega-information, hyper-connected society is through knowledge sharing. Smart partners know that sharing information is the currency of success and that building a collaborative culture to enable that to happen is the next logical step.

To accomplish this goal of sharing information, an organization needs to have in place a process that enables everyone to slow down under stress and be guided by leaders grounded in the personal mastery of being smart partners. Ideally, the organization infrastructure includes a grounded, compelling strategic framework, aligned strategies and tactics, agreements on priorities and allocation of resources, the right people with the right skills in the right jobs, and reward and compensation systems that drive the right behaviors. A plan must be in place to help people within the organization continue to hone their partnering skills, with the goal of making them smarter partners. Smarter than the competition.

THE POWERHOUSE PARTNER MODEL

The Powerhouse Partner Model, as shown in Figure 1, provides an end-to-end methodology comprising three key steps for turning a business into a Powerhouse Partner. All three are necessary for achieving the full potential and power of a partnering culture, the

FIGURE 1
Powerhouse Partner Model

To Build a Partnering Organization ...

TASK   **RELATIONSHIP**

❶

Practice Focused Leadership

- Attain personal mastery, inspire vision, motivate action, achieve results

❷

Build a Partnering Infrastructure

❸

Develop Smart Partners

- Create a strategic framework
- Redesign your organization as a partnering network
- Hire people with partnering competencies
- Keep and grow smart partners

- Reinforce the foundation for openness
  - Self-Disclosure and Feedback
  - Ability to Trust
- Move to the future with creativity
  - Future Orientation
  - Comfort with Change
- Embrace connectivity for agility
  - Win-Win Orientation
  - Comfort with Interdependence

Partnering Culture

An enabling organization culture competitively positioned to thrive
in the 21st-century information and connection economy

Outcomes:

- Free flow of information
- Customer satisfaction through relationship capabilities
- Lean horizontal structure based on network architecture
- Marketplace agility
- Innovation in application
- Abundance mentality in increasing value of human assets and strategic partners

foundation of a partnering organization. Each step involves specific objectives described in fuller detail in this and later chapters.

Practice Focused Leadership

The first step in building a partnering culture needs to be taken by an organization's executive leaders. Leaders must move beyond intellectually understanding partnering behaviors into living them on a daily basis. Partnering behaviors are a set of actions that build trust and inspire a sense of vision and confidence in others. These behaviors are what we have described as the Six Partnering Attributes:

- Self-Disclosure and Feedback

- Win-Win Orientation

- Ability to Trust

- Future Orientation

- Comfort with Change

- Comfort with Interdependence

When used consistently within the organization, these sets of partnering behaviors create the atmosphere that allows a partnering culture to thrive.

The executive team must purposefully decide they are going to behave in an open and trusting manner and commit to using the interpersonal behaviors described in the Six Partnering Attributes. Leaders must next hold each other accountable to practice the behaviors on which they have agreed. In addition to helping leaders set good examples, the Six Partnering Attributes provide a language that enables team members to communicate better with each other about which behaviors are productive and which are counterproductive. Through ongoing dialogue, language is bonded to action, building trust, sending positive charges through the atmosphere, and energizing the culture. Consequently, when people in a partnering culture talk about working collaboratively and building trust, members know what actions they must take to meet others' expectations. Over time, these partnering practices become behavioral norms embedded within the organization culture itself. They become "how things are done around here." They become the culture.

Build a Partnering Infrastructure

The second step in creating a partnering culture is to be sure the organization's infrastructure supports collaboration. When a compensation structure, for example, rewards counterproductive behaviors, people will display those counterproductive behaviors. People will do what they are paid to do, not what leaders preach they are expected to do. If you want collaborative behavior, you must balance the reward for both collaborative behavior and individual contribution. If you value trust, you must measure trust and reward it. It's not difficult, but few organizations have such behavioral measurements in place.

Develop Smart Partners

Once leaders have attained personal mastery using the Six Partnering Attributes, and once organization structures are in place to support the use of these attributes, employees must be trained on using them to accomplish work tasks. This continuous strengthening of partnering behaviors creates a self-reinforcing network and embeds the partnering language and the behaviors deeper and deeper within the organization. Ultimately, language turns into action, as partnering norms evolve into "how things are done around here."

ACHIEVING TASKS AND BUILDING RELATIONSHIPS

Creating a partnering culture using the Powerhouse Partner Model requires that you invest time, money, and energy both in achieving tasks and in building relationships. This task–relationship balance constitutes a central partnering dynamic that must always be in the forefront of a leader's mind. Traditional organizations are steeped in task, and in fact the task arena is where traditional leaders feel most comfortable. It is amazing, the reaction we get from leaders when we suggest that they just bring balance to the task and relationship dynamic within their organization. The blank stares say it all. To these leaders, relationships are of little value and do not produce "real work." They see relationship building as "touchy-feely" stuff.

Shifting from task to relationship feels counterintuitive and unnatural and is, consequently, viewed as unproductive and undervalued by these executives.

The act of transforming an organization culture, a paradox in itself, is messy and complex and requires leaders to exemplify their strongest relationship skills. Transforming an organization culture is like remodeling a kitchen. It's hard. It's messy. It takes longer and costs more than you thought. It will test the limits of your patience. You will ask, "Is this worth it?" But you can't slam the door in the face of the work crews and wish—presto!—for a clean countertop. Ain't gonna happen. You must push the boundaries of your patience with people. Unfortunately for many businesses, it's at this point that every instinct signals people to hunker down and get back to task at the expense of the relationship. Yelling at the contractor to get the kitchen done quicker won't make it happen. Screaming only irritates work crews, and then they work slower. No, this is the time to build that relationship and look for the win-win solution. Please understand, we are not suggesting that you take your eye off task achievement. After all, sticking to mission is an imperative, and serving customers well is paramount, but building internal relationships and modeling expected partnering behaviors is key to long-term transformation of an organization's culture. And building relationships takes additional effort on the part of senior leaders, an effort that may not reap benefits within the next quarter.

THE DIFFERENCE BETWEEN LEADING PEOPLE AND MANAGING A BUSINESS

Leaders must differentiate between leading people and managing production and transaction processes. These two disciplines require different sets of competencies. Leadership requires relationship skills, while management requires analytical and problem-solving skills. People often confuse the two sets of skills, sometimes with disastrous results. Both must be coordinated and aligned if the organization is to achieve its full potential. Over the past half-century or so, there's been a movement toward treating human resources as expendable commodities while concentrating on the tasks of the business. This imbalance in the dynamics of organizations has created soulless entities where people no longer feel valued, and employee, and thus customer, loyalty continues to decline. Why?

Two powerful forces, *material output* and *ethereal energy,* make up the heart and soul of every organization. The heart pumps life throughout the enterprise, delivering vital nutrients needed to get the job completed. The soul, however, gives the business its "life force," its unique imprint on the world, the source of its creativity and intelligence, defining the essence of its being. The Holistic Organization Model (see Figure 2) depicts the interrelationship between material output and ethereal energy in an organization.

The Holistic Organization Model offers a systematic approach for grasping the interconnected aspects of business strategies and serves as a mechanism for facilitating alignment across a company. The model integrates the two distinct realms—ethereal and material—that influence and reflect on each other. Ethereal energies, like the unseen influence of the moon on tides, powerfully drive organization performance. The material outputs result from shaped ethereal energies. Ethereal energies cascade with human motivation and potential, while material outputs entail transactions, products, and services. People watch closely for nonverbal behavioral clues establishing the boundaries of "right" and "wrong." Thus, any organization culture derives directly from the vision, values, and ethics demonstrated by its leaders. Culture defines what, how, when, and why we do what we do, thus becoming a backdrop to organization performance. The outcomes of a business's strategies and tactics are its products and services, its material outputs, tangible evidence of the organization's vision, values, and ethics.

Human energy is the most powerful energy in any organization. It is the vision, values, passion, and commitment of individuals that propel an organization to achieve great things. A leader's most important role is motivating, harnessing, and directing human energy to achieve the objectives of the organization. Leaders must be skilled in leading people by understanding their intrinsic motivators. Leaders must connect with people's core values to create the conditions and environment for people to achieve the objectives of the business. The result of this leadership is culture. For an organization to survive, it

FIGURE 2
Holistic Organization Model

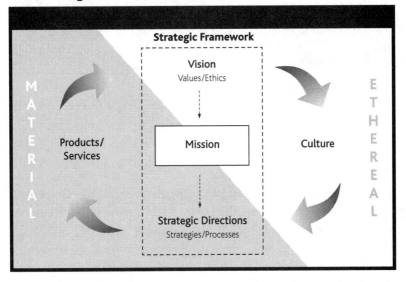

must produce something of value, something that is needed or wanted. The output of an organization ensures that the organization will have a purpose for its existence. Leaders manage material output. Specific steps designed to stabilize and control the production process ensure the desired outcomes.

Examples of Ethereal Energy

Ethereal energies are the unseen forces that drive organizations. These energies are based on, and reflect, the levels and quality of interaction between the people within the organization. Ethereal energies result directly from a leader's ability to create an organizational environment that supports and encourages human achievement. Ethereal energies are difficult to quantify. As with the wind, you know it's there when you feel it on your face, and you can see its impact, such as a flag waving or leaves blowing, but you can't actually see it. A good barometer for determining the quality of the ethereal energies in your organization is morale. Is the morale in your group high or low? Elements that contribute to the quality of ethereal energy include:

- Free and open communication

- People feeling valued

- People being listened to and leaders acting on their input

- People feeling like winners

- A dynamic organization

- A sense of team spirit and loyalty

Examples of Material Output

Material output directly reflects the ethereal energy within an organization. It also depends on the level of management skills demonstrated by leaders. These skills include strategic and tactical planning, process and project management, research, product and business development, sales and marketing, and other task-related management competencies. Well-managed organizations have such characteristics in common. These traits have become benchmarked both nationally in quality awards such as the Malcolm Baldrige National Quality Award (MBNQA) and internationally with ISO series certifications and others. Elements that contribute to the quality of material output include:

- A grounded, compelling strategic framework

- Aligned tactics and processes

- A defined process management system and scorecard

- Creative problem-solving technologies

- Uniform project management methodologies

Although the short-term effect of an imbalance between achieving tasks (management) and building relationships (leadership) may seem insignificant, the long-term impact on a business can be deadly. In the 1970s and '80s, factory workers for the "Big Three" American automobile manufacturers drove the cars they assembled. In fact, the first few employees that started arriving in employee parking lots in "foreign" cars were threatened, and their cars sometimes bashed . . .

figuratively, or literally, or both. Today, go to any of those employee parking lots and you will see a rainbow of makes and models. Employees no longer feel bound to purchase a car from their own employer. While the type of car an employee drives may not appear to mean much, the messages sent to consumers everywhere are extraordinarily powerful. "Even we don't drive the cars we build . . . Why should you?" This disconnect is an example of the potent force of ethereal energy. The messages are communicated and reverberate throughout the nation and businesses slowly die.

The American auto industry is in a thirty-year decline. According to Michael Ellis in a August 1, 2003, Reuters report, "Auto Sales Hit 2003 High—Big Three Fall," General Motors, Ford Motor Company, and Chrysler of Daimler-Chrysler lost 15 percent of the total market share in 2003, while Mercedes, the German division of Daimler-Chrysler, gained 20.6 percent, BMW gained 10.1 percent, and Audi gained 7 percent. All three Japanese manufacturers posted strong increases. Do Americans really build inferior cars, or do people believe Americans build inferior cars? In a relatively short time, the American automobile industry has managed to squander a century of employee and customer goodwill to satisfy the demands of a short-term bottom line by ignoring, at best, the human element of its business.

In the information-rich, interconnected world of the twenty-first century, organizations can no longer risk alienating either employees or customers by failing to connect with human values. Instead, they must balance the need to accomplish tasks while connecting with people's values, emotions, and desires—their human energy. To make this connection, the first step is to have leaders who create an environment that is open and receptive to partnering with others. Creating a partnering culture requires focused leadership to establish trust and open communication, listen to others' needs, and act on those needs.

Leaders have always played a pivotal role in shaping the culture of an organization. In the Dual Age of Information and Connections, the behaviors of leaders have become vital for success, and counterproductive leadership behaviors can have a severe, sometimes catastrophic, impact on the viability of an enterprise. Consider what happened at Enron, WorldCom, ImClone, Arthur Andersen, and other companies betrayed by self-indulgent executives. Mull over the trading scandals in the mutual fund industry. Reflect on the number of people hurt by the greed of certain C-suite brigands, schemers, and narcissists. Leaders who decide to commit to creating a partnering culture within their enterprise must also pledge themselves to lead by example, to model the Six Partnering Attributes. Leaders must take the first step by practicing focused leadership. In Chapter 4, we discuss step 1 of the Powerhouse Partner Model, "Practice Focused Leadership," and offer concrete suggestions for achieving the four objectives of focused leadership: attaining personal mastery, inspiring vision, motivating action, and achieving results.

4

Attaining Personal Mastery, Inspiring Vision, Motivating Action, Achieving Results

As my litter was borne to the rear my hat was placed over my face, and soldiers by the road-side said, "He is dead, and they are telling us he is only wounded." Hearing this repeated from time to time, I raised my hat with my left hand, when the burst of voices and the flying of hats in the air eased my pains somewhat.

—JAMES LONGSTREET, *FROM MANASSAS TO APPOMATTO*

Strong leaders build healthy cultures. To make a positive and productive impact on human activity, leaders must model the partnering behaviors they expect from others. People look at what leaders do rather than at what they say. The adage "walk the talk" seems more relevant than ever, as people have become more communication savvy as a result of being constantly barraged by media messages and political spin. People have learned to filter the disingenuous and inauthentic rhetoric that is passed off as the truth to decipher the hidden meanings and realities of convoluted messaging by looking for congruity with behavior. When they see congruity, they tend to believe in the authenticity of the individual and the message. When they see contradiction, they tend to dismiss them both.

POWERHOUSE PARTNER MODEL STEP 1: PRACTICE FOCUSED LEADERSHIP

What are the leadership qualities that can build this congruity between your words and actions? You must start by understanding yourself; you must be able to demonstrate the qualities you expect others to emulate. You must practice focused leadership and fulfill the four objectives described in the Powerhouse Partner Model.

Attain Personal Mastery

Knowing yourself—your strengths and weaknesses—in both inter-personal and technical competencies is the foundation of leadership. Being grounded in your values gives you a powerful voice of confidence and conviction. Understanding and being comfortable with who you are as a human being puts others at ease and makes you approachable. Leaders grounded in personal mastery lead by example, not by power or position. Leaders attain personal mastery by

- Having an accurate understanding of personal strengths and weaknesses

- Using an open, honest, direct, and candid communication style

- Being receptive to positive and constructive feedback

- Knowing inherent conflict styles and striving for win-win solutions
- Building emotional security
- Understanding personal technical capabilities
- Being realistic about personal work habits
- Building networks and partnerships
- Knowing limitations both interpersonally and technically
- Seeking input when problem solving
- Keeping commitments
- Seeking interaction with colleagues
- Trusting that others have good intentions
- Focusing on future events
- Understanding personal need for control and boundaries
- Being compassionate and expressing empathy for others
- Working collaboratively with others
- Being comfortable linking personal success with team success

Inspire Vision

Envisioning a future that is grander than self and having a noble cause that excites others are vital leadership goals. Being open to possibilities and aligning those opportunities with others who have a shared vision create commitment and lead to action. Trailblazing builds trust and inspiration, resulting in unlimited possibilities and growth. Leaders inspire vision by

- Knowing their passion
- Identifying a big theme
- Expressing themselves in future-oriented language
- Imagining possibilities
- Communicating using future-focused imagery

- Appealing to the senses

- Using powerful and compelling language

- Acting as if the future were today

- Dreaming the big dream

- Including others in the future

- Appealing to the common interest

- Looking outside the organization, industry, geographic area

- Being bold

Motivate Action

Exciting people to achieve more than they thought possible, aligning tasks in ways that deliver unexpected benefits, and opening the door to influence from others create momentum and a compelling case for action. Rewarding collaboration, fostering interdependence, and creating networks and information-sharing environments exponentially increase task output and quality. Being an active listener and embracing vulnerability and empathy endear you to others and ensure their commitment to achieving agreed-to results. Leaders motivate action by

- Aligning activities with the strategic framework

- Sharing information

- Listening to and acting on input

- Encouraging experimentation and innovation

- Building trust

- Removing fear

- Sharing opportunities for everyone to benefit personally

- Rewarding solutions-based behaviors

- Removing obstacles

- Providing resources

- Giving visible support and reinforcement
- Creating learning opportunities for self and others
- Creating reasons for inclusion
- Recognizing and expressing appreciation for others' work
- Creating collaborative rewards
- Recognizing successful teams

Achieve Results

Being tenacious, setting high expectations, and communicating that goals are achievable deliver results. Exceptional leaders focus on achievements and learn from mistakes. They share power and information while letting go of control. They embolden people to take measured strategic risks and reward them regardless of the outcome. They build accountability into the organization using techniques that encourage individuals to take accountability, rather than subjecting them to a finger-pointing culture. Leaders achieve results by

- Providing clear expectations
- Setting high and achievable standards
- Planning for and expecting success
- Reinforcing shared benefits
- Understanding and managing process excellence
- Measuring and monitoring with passion
- Turning the organization into a problem-solving powerhouse
- Developing a culture of accountability
- Starting with small, calculated steps
- Using the external network as required
- Establishing a learning center
- Coaching and being coached

- Recognizing, rewarding, and thanking others

- Cheerleading

Leaders must demonstrate daily the partnering behaviors needed to create cultures that thrive on open, positive communication and win-win problem-solving and conflict resolution strategies—cultures that are future focused, adaptable, and interdependent. Leaders must walk the partnering talk. As a leader, you must demonstrate the Six Partnering Attributes:

- *Self-Disclosure and Feedback* refers to providing others with information about yourself, addressing your needs, listening to others and their needs, and providing feedback to others on how their needs, actions, or behaviors affect you.

- *Win-Win Orientation* refers to seeking a win-win outcome to problem solving and conflict resolution. It also reflects on your ability to manage your emotions, defer self-gratification for the good of others, and negotiate successful outcomes.

- *Ability to Trust* refers to having confidence that you and others will do as promised and will behave in a straightforward manner. You can instill trust in others by having the capability to assess mistrust, address the issues, and rebuild trust between people.

- *Future Orientation* refers to focusing on a vision of the future and setting your expectations with that vision in mind. It also requires you to be open and accepting of new ideas.

- *Comfort with Change* refers to the extent to which you accept, adapt to, and even embrace change. A hallmark of effective leadership is the ability to introduce required change in the organization without alienating too many people.

- *Comfort with Interdependence* refers to relying on others for your success. The level of information needed to operate an organization is too complex for any one individual acting alone. Leaders know how to delegate and hold others accountable for results.

Of course demonstrating the Six Partnering Attributes is a lot harder than merely talking about it. John's story illustrates the difficulty some leaders have with walking the talk.

WALKING THE PARTNERING TALK— JOHN'S STORY

In an organization with a long history, John, a division CEO, knew that the existing bureaucratic culture was preventing his division from getting where it needed to go. He would constantly bemoan the inefficiencies he and his staff endured due to the nature of the parent organization. John felt that he had no control or influence over the culture, but, as we examined with him the objectives of focused leadership described earlier, John had to acknowledge that he did not live up to the ideals to which he aspired. Part of the problem, according to John, was that while he intellectually understood what it took to be a great leader, he kept getting sucked into the political whorls of the larger culture. Since his was just one of ten divisions, he felt it was impossible for him to make an impact on the larger culture, and so he stopped trying.

The reality was that John didn't want to challenge himself to be a great leader. He felt secure enough and at a high enough level within the organization to have a personal sense of accomplishment and satisfaction. He didn't want to rock the boat within the larger, politically sensitive organization and risk losing everything he had worked so hard to gain. He honestly believed he was a good leader and that people had confidence in him. But actually the only person he was fooling was himself. People within the division knew that John was a weak leader and one of the reasons the organization continued to stagnate and was beset with newsmaking mistakes and inquiries. In fact, John wanted to maintain the culture the way it was. Since there was no individual accountability, John never was concerned about being held accountable for his lack of leadership.

The story of John's reluctance to walk the partnering talk concludes the discussion of step 1 of the Powerhouse Partner Model, "Practice Focused Leadership." We now move on to step 2 of the model, "Build a Partnering Infrastructure," a task-intensive process that involves four distinct but interconnected objectives. We suggest in Chapter 5 an approach for creating a strategic framework and subsequently address the question of organization structure, the first two objectives of building a partnering infrastructure. In Chapter 6 we tackle the third challenge: how to hire people with partnering competencies. Then in Chapter 7 we complete step 2 of the Powerhouse Partner Model by offering suggestions for how leaders can keep and grow smart partners, the fourth objective of building a partnering infrastructure.

5

Redesigning Your Organization As a Partnering Network

We judge each other harshly and often unfairly. We do not credit that other people are more complex than they may seem to our small-minded view of them. Marriages break up because of this delusion, employees do not work well, and we needlessly separate ourselves from the talents offered by others.

—ROBERT ORNSTEIN, *MULTIMIND*

How many of us have ever thought about the source of the word *organization?* Its root likely derives from two Greek words—*organon,* tool or instrument, and *ergon,* work—implying a grouping of organisms working together as a means of accomplishing something. People might think of organizations as heartless, legal entities, but they are purposeful beings, much like plants and animals such as ourselves. Organizations experience the same needs, threats, and life cycles that other species do. So, if organizations live and die much as any other organism, why have we gotten into the habit of designing most of them as buildings?

POWERHOUSE PARTNER MODEL STEP 2: BUILD A PARTNERING INFRASTRUCTURE

Leadership by itself does not make a great organization. Great leaders have been brought to their knees by dysfunctional, misaligned, and entrenched bureaucracies encumbered by years of mismanagement.

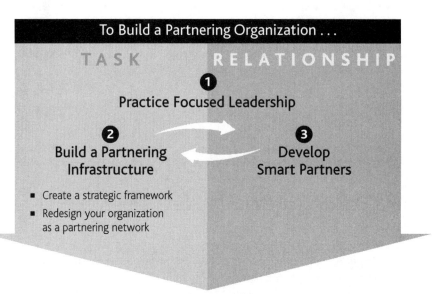

Partnering Culture

Structure often evolves haphazardly based on power and control, and budget and headcount rule. Little attention is given to how the parts of an organization structure interact, and alignment is commonly an afterthought.

Strategic Framework

The first step in building a partnering infrastructure is to create a grounded, compelling strategic framework (see the Holistic Organization Model, p. 47). This organizational framework interconnects the ethereal energies with the material outputs, creating an interactive, self-reinforcing system. A strategic framework has three principal components:

- Vision

- Mission

- Strategic directions

A vision statement describes the desired destiny of the organiza-tion—not a point on a timeline, but rather a navigational reference point guiding the business for the long haul. A vision is a "guiding star," not an *X* on a map. A short, compelling description of a valued outcome, a vision reflects the passion of the stakeholders and defines the meaning they give to their enterprise. It is buttressed by the values and ethics espoused by the organization's leaders as mani-fested in the behavior they demonstrate to others. For example, the vision for the U.S. Army reads in part, "Soldiers on point for the Nation . . . persuasive in peace, invincible in war." 3M's vision is, "To be the most innovative enterprise and the preferred supplier." FedEx's is, "Committed to a People-Service-Profit philosophy." The vision is the compelling force that drives the mission, thus linking the ethereal energies to the material outputs in the form of strategies, tactics, and processes. Excellence is achieved when alignment occurs between and within these forces and people's energies are connected to what they do on a daily basis.

A mission statement describes how an organization will achieve its vision. The mission identifies an enterprise's area of expertise and may target a specific industry or population. The mission of the U.S. Army is to "find peaceful solutions to the frictions between nations, address the problems of human suffering, and when required, fight and win our Nation's wars" (abridged). When Dell was Dell Computer, its mission was, "To be the most successful com-puter company in the world at delivering the best customer experi-ence in the markets we serve." Nordstrom consolidates its vision and mission into one statement: "Offer the customer the best possible service, selection, quality, and value."

A strategic direction specifies a broad area of organizational focus, the specific things the company needs to do over the next two to three years to achieve its mission. Collectively, an enterprise's strategic directions define at a high level how the organization intends to allocate its resources (people, money, time, technology). Often, strategic directions fall into one or more of three categories: customers, products and services, and operations. Here are some examples of strategic directions:

- Deliver national solutions through next-generation broadband networks

- Achieve end-to-end management of customer experience by end of year

- Deliver market-leading content, application, and Internet services in targeted markets within eighteen months

Following is a case study about a telecommunications company that concluded that it needed to create a new strategic framework.

CASE STUDY: A TELECOMMUNICATIONS COMPANY

Creating a Strategic Framework

A large telecommunications company launched a wireless division in the late 1990s. The specific goal was to achieve a market share position of number one or number two in each of the markets it served within the first three years of business. The overriding challenge was to create an aggressive team that would break through the bureaucracy of a firmly established telecom company to win in a competitive marketplace. As it happened, the company attained a number two or number three position in most geographic markets within eighteen months. The executive team attributed its success to a superior product and, in part, to individual heroics and the entrepreneurial spirit of the wireless team.

In the third year, challenges began to emerge. Subscriber growth was slowing, and the market was becoming hypercompetitive. Prices were plummeting as each player matched the next in what seemed like a rapidly moving chess game. The company's focus blurred and the lack of processes began to strain the organization. In some instances, people were working at cross-purposes. The company needed to be reenergized so that its entrepreneurial spirit could be sustained, but within the structure of an established organization moving out of a start-up mode toward profitability. Faced with this challenge, the executive team committed to redefining the purpose of the organization.

To ensure clarity of purpose, the executive team took the lead in defining and communicating a grounded, compelling strategic framework. The president elected to base the new strategic framework on the Holistic Organization Model. Communications, vision, and objectives had been transmitted easily up and down organizational lines when the company was small. But the adrenaline-driven growth organization was maturing into a complex company that needed to build employee loyalty while increasing subscriber satisfaction with its products and services. Leaders knew they needed a consistent message, but they did not agree on where the enterprise was going.

In a series of facilitated sessions—supplemented by subteam meetings and employee focus groups—the executive team developed a vision statement, mission statement, and strategic directions (see Table 4). It rolled out the strategic framework in face-to-face sessions with employees. Employees responded enthusiastically to the strategic framework, commenting on its simplicity, its power, and its boldness. Managers reacted more cautiously, however, wondering privately whether the executive team was "really serious" about building a global wireless communications business.

How the executive team went about creating the strategic framework offers practical instruction on executive dynamics. The main obstacle was getting sufficient time and energy from executives. It was overcome by using a series of facilitated half-day conversational meetings with the entire executive team—only for general discussions and for decisions. Three-person subteams guided by a facilitator met in iterative one-hour sessions to hash out precise wording for the vision, mission, and strategic directions. Having subteams prepare working drafts for discussion and decisions allowed the entire executive team to focus on reaching consensus on the big ideas. This multiple short-burst approach permitted the periods of incubation, testing, and retesting so crucial for building gut-level ownership of the final strategic framework.

TABLE 4

Strategic Framework for a Telecommunications Company (Sample)

Vision
Work together to make it possible for customers to communicate without limits

Mission
Achieve global leadership in wireless communications by delivering the solutions and experience that matter most to customers

Strategic Directions
Excel at customer experience and quality to drive acquisition and retention
Lead the industry in innovative technologies to accelerate growth in market share
Drive out unnecessary costs for reinvestment and faster EBITDA growth
Excel at cross-functional execution as the cornerstone of our competitive advantage

THE BENEFITS OF BEING A POWERHOUSE PARTNER

The kind of organization culture that made the developed world an industrial powerhouse after World War II—considered the starting point for mass industrialization—will not sustain businesses in the next economic age. The Dual Age of Information and Connections operates on fundamentally different principles from those of the Industrial Age. The industrial economy was based on the concept of scarcity and the conservation of material goods . . . resources of both the material and human varieties. Information becomes more valuable as it becomes abundant and, as it spreads, it can morph into something new, whereas a material product cannot. A car is a car, but an idea, a thought, a creative spark of genius can grow into unimaginable value. Imagine harnessing the brilliance of the workforce. Imagine learning from each other. Imagine networking intellectual capital and transforming it into satisfying customers' needs. Imagine having the agility of a gazelle and the ability to leap from consumer trend to consumer trend without a lag, leading the marketplace. Imagine being an innovation factory turning out new and exciting ideas and concepts on a regular basis. Imagine having a workforce that is not just loyal, but feels a sense of duty to the success of the organization.

These aspirations are not simply the compilations of an executive wish list. They are the requirements of a Powerhouse Partner in the Dual Age of Information and Connections. Once the leaders of an organization have established a grounded, compelling strategic framework, they must determine the degree to which the enterprise is structured in a manner that supports the company's partnering strategy going forward. Further, they must assess the degree to which the people in the organization currently demonstrate smart partnering behaviors.

Creating a grounded, compelling strategic framework and implementing a systematic partnering process are fundamental steps in building a partnering infrastructure, but they are not enough. Organization structure plays a key role in how effectively the human energy of a company is focused and directed. Traditional hierarchical organization designs institutionalize roadblocks to the flow of information and to the formation of connections. This limitation comes as no surprise in that hierarchy functions principally as an instrument of centralized control and risk avoidance. When resources are scarce, when assets depreciate, centralized control makes sense. But in a world in which our most vital resources—information and relationships—are appreciating assets, available in abundance, organization designs rooted in hierarchy are doomed to limp along, even fail. Partnering is a fusion reaction, not a fission reaction—that is, a coming together rather an exploding apart. Given that the highest purpose of organization structure is to connect people and resources to produce an end result, leaders who want their organization to become a Powerhouse Partner in the twenty-first century need to consider how their enterprise can be structurally reconfigured to that end.

WHY ORGANIZATION STRUCTURE MATTERS

An organization's structure describes how accountability for results and corresponding work tasks are distributed and managed in an enterprise. Responsibilities for outputs and task performance are clustered into jobs, jobs are grouped into larger and larger divisions, and divisions are arranged to drive the implementation of the organization's purpose. Moreover, an organization's structure must promote the efficient functioning of both its core business processes and enabling business processes and facilitate the effective deployment and development of its members. The central challenge in creating a new organization structure is to figure out which design best balances the *disconnection* that comes from distributing work with the *connection* required to focus all the organization's members on achieving its purpose together. For example, on one hand multiple management layers and narrow spans of control may be the most expedient means of controlling work and the resources needed to accomplish it, but on the other hand they may well make overall connection—and communication—within an organization difficult to attain.

Getting organization structure right is a tall order. Creating or changing an organization structure involves two interconnected activities: *job design* and *organization design*. Job design defines, sorts, and assigns the accountabilities and tasks derived from the outputs that must be produced by an organization's core and enabling processes. In addition, job design identifies the competencies— knowledge, skills, and abilities—required for an incumbent to perform at a high level. Accountabilities outline the "what" of a particular job's concrete results that contributes to achieving the enterprise's purpose. Competencies describe the "how" of that job in terms of the specific behaviors that drive outstanding performance.

Organization design creates an overall configuration that reflects vital interrelationships among discrete jobs and among groups of jobs. Design criteria for framing an organization structure are built from organizing principles, givens, and constraints, and a variety of both internal and external drivers. In short, design criteria must flow out of an organization's strategic framework: its vision, mission, and strategic directions. From the point of view of inherent design logic, an organization can be structured by customers, products, processes, strategic objectives, functions, territories, networks, and other dimensions, as well as by combinations of these dimensions, that is, a matrix or lattice. Of course the "right" structure does not guarantee success. Yet, the "wrong" structure can fracture an organization, isolate

units and individuals, insulate management, block communication, .
and spark the flare-up of dysfunctional subcultures that undercut the
organization's purpose. A structure that conflicts with an organization's vision, undermines its mission, or contradicts its strategic
directions serves only to confuse, frustrate, and in the long run para-
lyze its members. An enterprise's organization structure must be
aligned with its strategic framework.

In a case study of the creation of a world-class supply-chain
organization, beginning on the following page, we see how a partnering organization can become the vehicle for implementing a smart
partnering strategy. In part 1 of this five-part case, we discuss the
vital link between developing a partnering strategy and then building
a partnering organization to implement that strategy.

How an organization decides to structure itself has long-lasting
implications for the competencies required to make that structure
work, day in and day out. If, for example, a company wishes to "de-
layer" and broaden "spans of control," it will need to select candidates who display a specific set of competencies such as initiative,
ownership and accountability, and risk taking. You don't enter a
Clydesdale in the Kentucky Derby, and you do not strap Secretariat
into a plow harness.

Here's the bottom line. If, as we have asserted, partnering is
emerging as an essential business strategy for the twenty-first century,
the Dual Age of Information and Connections, what are the implications of embracing a partnering philosophy on the structure of an
organization? How might organizations be shaped differently not
only to allow or even encourage partnering, but also to *drive* partnering as "how things are done around here"? That is, how do we use
structure to help create a partnering culture?

THE PARTNERING PARADOX IN JOB DESIGN

If partnering is to become "how things are done around here," it
must be baked into every job. It thus must be included as a "job
spec," a historically documented criterion in a job description. In
some jobs partnering may well turn out to be the overriding job spec,
that is, the aspect of the position that creates the greatest value for

PARTNERING ORGANIZATION CASE STUDY: CREATING A WORLD-CLASS SUPPLY-CHAIN ORGANIZATION

Part 1: A Bold Strategy

A midsized global manufacturer with $1 billion-plus annual revenue wanted to create a world-class supply-chain organization—a source of distinct competitive advantage. The president's vision for the organization included the purchasing function becoming the mirror image of the company's sales organization. As he explained:

> *Our purchasing professionals have the ability to impact the bottom line as much as if not more than our sales people. They must work with our suppliers as closely as our sales people work with our customers to build lasting partnerships. The global contracts that they negotiate for materials and services for our worldwide manufacturing plants have a huge impact on our profits. To be a successful global competitor, we must contain costs. In our case, this is particularly important, since 70 percent of our costs are related to the procurement of materials and services. The only difference between the two groups is that one does the buying and the other does the selling.* (emphasis added)

This innovative supply-chain strategy called for a completely different kind of purchasing organization, one staffed with highly skilled negotiators focused on partnering with suppliers worldwide in implementing global procurement strategies. The challenge was that the purchasing group lacked the organization structure and the internal credibility it needed to drive strategic decisions within the company.

So, the president established a new mission: to build a partnering organization that would create procurement strategies to utilize the company's supplier base as a key resource for distinct competitive advantage. A cross-functional structure team with members from Marketing, Engineering, Manufacturing, and Purchasing was chartered to design the new structure. Facilitated by Jim Krefft, co-author of this book, the structure team was personally charged by the president to think "outside the box" in examining the current organization structure and analyzing customary purchasing processes. Within a week, the group developed a new structural framework for the procurement organization, creating an innovative partnering network and redefining the roles of purchasing professionals.

To date, the company has saved over $400 million in procurement activities as a result of the partnering organization redesign initiative that was driven by the new supply-chain strategy.

the enterprise. But this criterion presents a paradox, because partnering is both a job input and a job output. Partnering comprises both a set of behavioral characteristics (an input for which we can interview and hire, as detailed in Chapter 6) and produces the outputs (products and services and strategic alliances) an organization needs to accomplish its purpose. Partnering is thus

- A performance competency—a set of interconnected behaviors

- An accountability—a series of tasks that produces business results

- A relationship output—partnerships, arrays of relationships

All three of these facets of partnering yield two vital organizational assets that can appreciate over time: information and relationships. However, conventional formats for job descriptions—position descriptions, position profiles—are not as a rule configured to incorporate this partnering paradox as a job criterion. Typical formats serve the traditional purpose of job descriptions—to justify job level and compensation, and by extension to control payroll expense—and as such they have served more as a human resources audit document and a headcount management billy club than as a practical management tool for line managers. A partnering organization needs a more flexible tool.

Any enterprise that wishes to tackle the challenge of creating a partnering organization must at some point examine both its current job evaluation system—how it pegs jobs for pay—and the existing templates it uses for writing job descriptions. If you believe that partnering creates immense ongoing value for an organization, then those jobs that are accountable for forging, managing, and growing partnerships must be valued, and the incumbents compensated, accordingly. People generally do what they think they are being paid to do. It is common to "pay for performance." If you want a partnering organization, you had better be willing to "pay for partnering." If you do not, it will not happen. Organizations do not partner, people partner. Let's see how this principle worked in part 2 of the partnering organization case study.

PARTNERING ORGANIZATION CASE STUDY: CREATING A WORLD-CLASS SUPPLY-CHAIN ORGANIZATION

Part 2: Job Design

The partnering network began to fall into place after the structure team conceived of a new kind of position, the supply manager. The authority and responsibility of the new position were to equal those of a sales manager position. Both have managerial responsibilities. Supply managers manage partnerships with vendors, and sales managers manage partnerships with customers. In addition, both have authority over pricing. Supply managers approve vendor prices, while sales managers approve contract prices with customers. This new job design was completely different from the company's traditional purchasing organization philosophy.

The structure team also created another new position, supply service representative, to act as a day-to-day interface between vendors and plants, between plants and sales managers, and among the various supply management teams. Similar to a sales and service organization that has administrative and logistical support from customer service representatives, the structure team concluded that supply managers needed the same kind of professional support: to research vendors and pricing, to expedite paperwork, to troubleshoot procurement bottlenecks, and to keep sales managers up to date on the status of their customers' orders. A supply service representative supports each supply management team.

In creating innovative job designs to drive smart partnering, the main obstacle for leaders is that most job evaluation policies and practices now in place are deeply rooted in a command-and-control philosophy and its corollary, "bigger is better." The biggerer, the betterer. Positions involving greater numbers of customers, higher revenue, larger capital and expense budgets, more people, and greater territory are evaluated at higher levels, whatever job evaluation algorithm (point factor, benchmark, and so on) an organization's compensation gurus choose to employ to "value" jobs. The name of the salary advancement game is to increase the scope of one's job— and everybody knows it. Without question, quantitative scope will continue to remain an indispensable factor in any job evaluation system, but going forward, partnering must also become a major factor in job evaluations. Partnering creates value; people partner; pay for partnering.

Lip service to the value of smart partnering is easy, but making partnering a vital part of how we do business every day is much more difficult. To institutionalize partnering as a job evaluation factor, to make it a "BFOQ," a bona fide occupational qualification in affirmative action compliance lingo, the partnering requirements for a job must be built into the job description for that position. As a mechanism for accomplishing this aim, here are two suggestions: first, incorporate a Partnering Profile as an integral part of the job description for any position for which partnering is a critical enterprise activity; and second, add a Partnering Summary section to the job description for each position in the organization. Of course for bargaining unit positions, leaders may have to negotiate such changes with union members and leaders. Let's elaborate on these two suggestions for institutionalizing partnering in your organization.

Partnering Profile

In addition to "tombstone" data (job title, "reports to," etc.) and signature blocks, a standard job description by and large consists of three sections: a summary (including minimum requirements); a list of accountabilities (responsibilities, outputs, or activities); and selection criteria (competencies, or knowledge, skills, and abilities). Parsing out partnering among these customary sections of a job description would serve only to dilute an organization's emphasis on partnering. Rather than divide the partnering requirements among the summary, accountabilities, and selection criteria sections, add a Partnering Profile as a stand-alone section in the job descriptions for those positions that require substantive partnering skills and results. The Partnering Profile shown in Figure 3 is divided into three parts to mirror the three facets of partnering mentioned earlier: partnerships, partnering accountabilities, and partnering competencies. Keeping the partnering facets together emphasizes their interconnection and their significance for organizational success.

Partnering Summary

For positions that do not require substantive partnering skills and results, we suggest that general partnering requirements be incorporated either as a stand-alone section in a job description (see Figure 4)—perhaps just beneath the position summary—or as a subsection of the position summary section (see Figure 5). In the latter case, use subheads to call special attention to the particularly unique job specifications relating to partnering. Partnering must come to be viewed as part of "my real job."

A PARTNERING NETWORK

Reconfiguring job descriptions to incorporate the three dimensions of partnering is a first step but is in itself insufficient to institutionalize partnering. The next step in ensuring that an organization's structure is aligned both with its partnering philosophy and with its partnering processes is to redesign the enterprise as a partnering network. How a particular partnering network looks on paper will of course vary from organization to organization, but we would like to lay out suitable design criteria for a partnering organization and then offer a collaborative process for going about the work of building a partnering network. But remember: A partnering culture is a governing organization culture intended to optimize interconnections among an enterprise's various subcultures, which are sometimes at odds with one another. Furthermore, building a partnering network is not a new incarnation of "reengineering."

FIGURE 3
Partnering Profile

Partnerships: List vital partnerships incumbent must build, maintain, or expand; link partnerships to business goals and objectives.

External:

Internal:

Partnering Accountabilities: List 2–3 key partnering results incumbent must achieve; link partnering results to business targets.

1.

2.

3.

Partnering Competencies: Identify the partnering knowledge, skills, and abilities required to accomplish the partnering accountabilities. Describe each partnering competency as it relates to this position and to the partnerships listed above.

Self-Disclosure and Feedback:

Win-Win Orientation:

Ability to Trust:

Future Orientation:

Comfort with Change:

Comfort with Interdependence:

FIGURE 4

Partnering Summary As a Stand-Alone Section of Job Description

SECTION *X*: PARTNERING SUMMARY
Partnering Contributions: Describe in general terms how incumbent must partner day to day, internally and externally; link partnering contributions to strategic goals and to business targets.
Partnering Competencies: Identify briefly in behavioral terms the partnering knowledge, skills, and abilities required to make the partnering contributions listed above; as needed, reference the Six Partnering Attributes™: Self-Disclosure and Feedback, Win-Win Orientation, Ability to Trust, Future Orientation, Comfort with Change, and Comfort with Interdependence.

Building a partnering network involves mainly *overlaying* the partnering network atop the existing organization structure. We are not necessarily talking about massive, top-to-bottom organizational surgery, although in certain instances that degree of structural redesign might, for other sound business reasons, be in order. A partnering network is a structure that formally connects the organization's members based on the internal relationships required to accomplish a particular task. Thus, partnering networks overlay departmental boundaries, enabling the enterprise to achieve its strategic goals. For example, engineers partner with marketers to bring products to the marketplace. Design in ways to make it easy for

FIGURE 5
**Partnering Summary As Part of a Position Summary
Section of Job Description**

SECTION X: POSITION SUMMARY
Position Overview: Describe the overall purpose of this position. Include main areas of responsibility and scope (e.g., number of customers, amount of annual revenue, size of capital and expense budgets, office/plant locations, and payroll).
Partnering Summary: Describe in general terms how incumbent must partner day to day; link partnering contributions to business targets. Identify partnering competencies required by referencing the Six Partnering Attributes™: Self-Disclosure and Feedback, Win-Win Orientation, Ability to Trust, Future Orientation, Comfort with Change, and Comfort with Interdependence. **Partnering Contributions:** **Partnering Competencies:**
Minimum Requirements: List minimum education and experience needed for this job. Include licenses or certifications required.

partners to meet and work face-to-face often. Time and distance are heartless, relentless adversaries. A company that aspires to prosper as a partnering organization has to configure itself so that the members of its most critical partnerships can connect with each other, almost without thinking, as often as they need to. Organizations do not partner; people partner.

MARKETPLACES AND PATHWAYS

Marketplaces and pathways, two of the essential design principles of a partnering network, have been around for tens of thousands of years. They are natural ways in which people connect with each other and exchange goods and services. In effect, a partnering network establishes an open platform for instituting and using the marketplaces and building and using the pathways necessary for rapid, repeatable, direct human interconnections. Although e-mail, cell phones, and wireless networks are the greatest things since fire for bringing people together, there's more to connecting than that. For people to forge, sustain, and grow smart partnerships, they must work face-to-face with some frequency. Ever try dating someone who lives a thousand miles away? Even one hundred miles away? Marketplaces and pathways form the foundation of a Powerhouse Partner.

Marketplaces

Marketplaces hinge on the nitty-gritty question "How do we get what we need?" As such, instituting the right mix of organizational marketplaces challenges us as both the simplest and the most difficult task in creating a partnering network, for we are now talking about people having to give and wanting to get. We have to get clear on what we want, and on how and when to ask for it. As important, we have to know what we can contribute, and how and when to best make that contribution. Basically, marketplaces are places where people exchange what they have—or what they can get—for what they need or want: public markets, trading pits, black markets, gray markets, bartering clubs, swap meets, family meetings, blackjack tables, lunch tables. Most of these different types of marketplaces exist in one form or another inside most organizations, particularly in large corporations, branches of the military, and government agencies. If an organization's leaders do not mold its marketplaces by design, they will take shape by evolution.

People are ever keen to find the exchange venue that best serves their needs and wants. The members of an organization are no different. It is in these arenas of exchange that the process and tools of smart partnering will yield their greatest value to an organization desiring to install a partnering culture. What's fair and what's not? Did you give me what you committed, and did I give you what I promised? How much do we trust each other to make things right if one of us goofs up? Without a systematic, neutral process for governing how exchanges take place and without tools for expediting trades and resolving disagreements, marketplaces are open to corruption, deceit, and greed. In the end it is an enterprise's marketplaces, external and internal, that will make or break any attempt to change an organization's culture. If people do not change how they behave, you have just spent a million dollars and a zillion hours to prove, once again, that culture rules.

Pathways

Pathways are another major material component of an organization's culture. Pathways get right at the practical question "How do we get there from here?" For an organization deciding whether to overhaul its culture, the construction of pathways forces an examination of the avenues your organization has taken historically, those used by your competitors, and new trails to be blazed, as well as shifting combinations of all three. The essential issue is not whether particular pathways, or combinations thereof, constitute the "right" way to go, but whether an organization's leaders agree on which to take—at least in the short term. An organization might choose any number of different paths to get to its destination, and likely will need to abandon old lanes and blaze, or find, new trails at a moment's notice.

Pathways embrace the core and enabling business processes, office locations, workstation design and arrangement, information technology, and so on. Here, the principal challenge for an organization's leaders is to interconnect these components and systems in a manner that produces both the sturdiness required to withstand marketplace shocks and the flexibility needed for ongoing alignment and readjustment. Yes, we know what has been preached, lo, these many years about alignment and integration—get everyone facing the same way, pointed in the same direction, keeping in view both your buddies on the left and on the right. The global business marketplace has already redefined what constitutes both alignment and integration. Compare, for example, how alignment and integration were used by British regulars during the American Revolutionary War with how they were used by the upstart colonial army. The British marched in regimented rows with military discipline, while colonialists hung in trees and hid in ditches. In the twenty-first century, global pathways are not straight, nor are they paved, nor are they long—rather they are short, twisting, and bumpy. In the Dual Age of Information and Connections pathways stretch and twirl, shimmy and shake. Nowadays, global pathways *dance*. A company wishing to become a partnering organization must create its own pathways that are likewise capable of dancing.

Read through part 3 of the partnering organization case study on the facing page to see how the principles of a partnering network were put into practice.

Design Criteria for Partnering Network—a Starter Set

To create a partnering network suitable for driving implementation of its strategic framework, an organization's leaders must first agree on a set of design criteria. These criteria cannot be dictated from the outside; they cannot be lifted directly from an organization design textbook; they cannot be copied from successful competitors. However, for an organization's structure to serve as a platform for partnering, it must be based on design criteria anchored in the Six Partnering Attributes. Here are some design criteria, so based, for transforming your enterprise into a partnering network:

- **Open architecture**—build for accessibility, transparency, and involvement (Self-Disclosure and Feedback)

- **Free substitution**—build so that people can easily find the partners they need, internally or externally (Win-Win Orientation)

- **Opportunity and ownership**—build both to give people choices and opportunities and to delineate clearly who is accountable for what results (Ability to Trust)

- **Creativity and innovation**—build for experimentation, risk taking, and tolerating mistakes (Future Orientation)

- **Plug, unplug, replug**—build connectors that can be quickly unhooked and refastened with minimum resources (Comfort with Change)

- **Boundarylessness**—borders that are both porous and pliable (Comfort with Interdependence)

PARTNERING ORGANIZATION CASE STUDY: CREATING A WORLD-CLASS SUPPLY-CHAIN ORGANIZATION

Part 3: A Partnering Network

Under the old procurement structure, the company's buyers, lead buyers, senior buyers, and managers had limited spans of pricing control and hard, preset guidelines that required three bids and multiple sign-offs before a purchase transaction could be authorized. At the heart of the company's procurement function was a traditional command-and-control management philosophy wherein buyers were in fact micromanaged by an overwhelming assembly of design engineers, plant engineers, plant materials managers, manufacturing operations managers, corporate finance officers, service parts managers, and so on. The existing structure of the procurement function reflected these tight management controls: spans of control in the procurement function were extremely narrow (1:2 on average), and the organization had four layers, with instances of one-on-one-on-one reporting relationships.

Two basic principles of organization design are (1) build from the bottom up and (2) staff from the top down. With the supply manager and supply service representative positions having been established as the key jobs of the company's new supply-chain organization, the overall functional structure took the shape of an interdependent, yet flexible, two-layer partnering network of tightly knit supply management teams. This structure replaced the multilayered organization and streamlined the decision-making process. The structure team felt that a traditional static, two-dimensional wiring diagram would be inadequate for depicting the robust, dynamic, and innovative concept of a partnering network. It created visual aids to illustrate the partnering relationships of the new supply-chain organization by

- Showing the new organization's day-to-day relationships with manufacturing plants worldwide

- Specifying how the supply management team would partner with vendors in various categories of goods and services

- Explaining how the redesigned procurement function would interact with key corporate functions such as parts and service, design engineering, and finance, as well as with the sales organization

ORGANIZATION STRUCTURE WORK PLAN

The work plan for designing a partnering network comprises seven key steps:

1. Determine design criteria for the partnering organization.

2. Brainstorm options for the partnering network.

3. Evaluate structure options.

4. Build the case for the recommended structure option.

5. Prepare new partnering organization charts.

6. Revise or write new job descriptions to include a Partnering Profile.

7. Prepare an implementation road map.

Let's examine each step in detail.

Step 1: Determine Design Criteria for the Partnering Organization

As suggested earlier, the first step in building a new organization structure is for the leadership team to agree on a set of specific design criteria for each department or function. For example, the leadership team may determine that the new organization should provide a centralized point of focus for stakeholder communications or identify a clear point of accountability for cost reduction and cost control, and so on. These specifications constitute the design criteria against which the options developed in step 2 will be evaluated. To arrive at this set of design criteria, we recommend that the leadership team conduct a series of facilitated discussions to consider the following factors:

- The organization's strategic framework: vision, mission, and strategic directions

- The Six Partnering Attributes: Self-Disclosure and Feedback, Win-Win Orientation, Ability to Trust, Future Orientation, Comfort with Change, and Comfort with Interdependence

- Business parameters and constraints and other external drivers such as competition, technology, legislation, and community impact

- Internal drivers such as entrenched operational practices, sunk costs, and legacy systems

- Benchmarks and best practices

An organization's purpose is the most important driver of an organization's structure. Typically the organization's leaders, usually with coaching, prepare a structure team charter outlining the team's scope, objectives, and so on. One of the key elements in this charter is a list of initial organizing principles, givens, and constraints that in effect draw the basic operational boundaries—what's on the table, what's off the table.

Step 2: Brainstorm Options for the Partnering Network

Once the leadership team has agreed on a set of design criteria, we suggest that it sponsor a steering committee to charter a structure team. This team performs the analyses required to determine how the jobs and functions of the organization would be best organized. The structure team may recruit additional employees (creating subteams) for their subject matter expertise to assist in the development of options. Structure team members will then brainstorm a variety of options for aligning the entire organization with the strategic framework and with the principles of smart partnering, consistent with the set of design criteria identified in step 1. Whether an organization chooses to do process improvements before, during, or after shaping a new structure depends on the organization's total portfolio of drivers for change, including core and enabling business processes, among others. In any event, the interconnection of structure with core and enabling processes is paramount, in that the old adage "form follows function" still applies. If not addressed before a structure team is chartered, process control, improvement, or design must be addressed once the structure team has completed its work.

Step 3: Evaluate Structure Options

The structure team next evaluates each alternative against the strategic framework, the principles of smart partnering, and the design criteria previously established. From this strategic analysis, the optimal organization structure will emerge.

Step 4: Build the Case for the Recommended Structure Option

To support the recommended option for a partnering network, the structure team prepares a business case to present first to the steering committee and later to the entire leadership team. The business case should include elements such as

- Opportunity synopsis

- Scope, assumptions, constraints

- Recommended structure(s)

- Targeted results and benefits

- Evidence: quantitative, qualitative

- Measures

- Risk assessment

- Initial implementation steps

Step 5: Prepare New Partnering Organization Charts

After the optimal organization structure has been developed, structure team members will recommend the size of each unit in the newly realigned organization.

Step 6: Revise or Write New Job Descriptions to Include a Partnering Profile

For first-level and second-level positions, the structure team will draft new job descriptions, including a Partnering Profile or a Partnering Summary (as described earlier).

Step 7: Prepare an Implementation Road Map

In assessing the proposed changes, the structure team must prepare a plan for successful transition and identify transition challenges—especially those that may directly affect immediate implementation of the new structure. For example, which units will experience the greatest change during the transition? Which critical business tasks may fall through the cracks during the transition if not appropriately addressed? Here are some categories of transition challenges that may need to be addressed in the implementation road map:

- **Leadership:** personal visibility, desired behaviors, commitment

- **Workload:** interim resources required, cross-functional support, nonimmediate tasks and objectives

- **Morale:** employee support, employee communication, leadership changes

- **Land mines:** major changes, hard-hit functions, critical business tasks, key employees, displaced employees, early warning signs

- **Staging areas:** nonimmediate implementation, phase-in plan, phase-out plan

- **Customers and other stakeholders:** customer information needs, internal stakeholder needs, external stakeholder needs, community impact, political ramifications

INSTITUTIONALIZING PARTNERING

An organization's structure, indeed every position within the organization, needs to be derived from and find meaning in the organization's purpose. The main purpose of structure is to connect people and resources in a manner that best enables achievement of an organization's strategic business objectives and that most quickly moves the organization toward its vision and values. Of course it also provides a mechanism for dividing up accountabilities and tasks, that is, who will do what when for whom. However, the highest purpose of structure is to act as a means of coordinating, focusing, and unifying the individual efforts of all the organization's members. Structure sets the framework for how an organization chooses to achieve its strategic business objectives. Direction without structure dissolves into aimlessness; structure without direction becomes rigid. Creating a viable partnering organization requires not only the embracing of a partnering philosophy and the adoption of a systematic partnering process, it also entails the creation of a partnering structure that is both loose and tight, fast and anchored, agile and solid.

In this chapter we have introduced the job design concepts of a Partnering Profile and a Partnering Summary and the organization design model of a partnering network. We have shown how a company can adopt, or adapt, these new ideas to align and integrate the day-to-day activities of the organization in a way that speeds the flow of information and optimizes the propagation of connections. What we have been talking about in sum is how to institutionalize partnering in the Dual Age of Information and Connections. Partnering creates value; people partner; build your organization for partnering; pay for partnering. And pick your partners. In Chapter 6 we discuss how you can use the Partnering Interview to identify and hire— more readily and reliably—people who already have the partnering competencies you need to create a partnering organization, to become a Powerhouse Partner.

6

Hiring People with Partnering Competencies

How absolute the knave is! We must speak by
the card, or equivocation will undo us.

—SHAKESPEARE, *HAMLET*

People build an organization's culture—not noble ideals, neat org charts, or nifty software. People build a culture through what they believe and what they value and how they treat each other, their partners, and their customers. It comes down to what they do on the job every day, and how they do what they do. To build a partnering culture, the leaders of a company must know what kinds of behaviors propel human connections and, by extension, which competencies drive those partnering behaviors.

Over the past two decades many companies have come to adopt competency-based assessment as the selection methodology of choice. Consulting organizations and corporate human resources departments have invested mightily in empirical research to determine which competencies drive behaviors associated with outstanding leadership and with technical proficiency at every level. What they have discovered is that most every company is in the hunt for the same kind of people, whether the organization is public or private, profit or nonprofit, large or small, regardless of industry segment or governmental agency. Unfortunately, enterprise leaders, corporate human resources executives, and behavioral scientists have spent far less effort on figuring out what kind of people an organization needs to build a partnering culture. What they should be trying to find are smart partners.

Partnering Culture

FINDING SMART PARTNERS

But what do smart partners look like? In the Dual Age of Information and Connections, companies must rethink the competencies they view as being core to their organization's culture and success. In the twenty-first century, smart partnering is emerging as one of the pre-eminent competencies needed for outstanding job performance—a linchpin that ties together all other workplace behaviors into an organic network of high-performance capability. These partnering-enabling competencies must form the foundation for an organization's human performance system going forward. Hiring people with these partnering competencies accelerates the building of a partnering culture, and thus a partnering organization. In this chapter we discuss the competencies that directly drive partnering behaviors and describe what it takes to identify these and other partnering competencies and to ensure their alignment with a strategic framework, the success of which hinges on smart partnering.

HIRING PEOPLE WITH PARTNERING COMPETENCIES

Finding people with partnering competencies, people who will drive a partnering culture, is crucial for reliability and sustainability in a company that aspires to become a Powerhouse Partner. Corporate charm schools nestled among pines and brooks cannot undo the ruin wreaked by a crummy selection. Lose-lose mis-hires can cripple a partnering organization and rapidly undo its investment in smart partnering. People with a scarcity mentality hatch underground plots to steal away resources and run from reasonable risks. Employees who resist change undermine creativity and responsiveness. Breeches of trust act as relationship wrecking balls. The cost of poor selection can be enormous.

This chapter introduces the concept of the Partnering Interview, an interviewing protocol we recommend in conjunction with structured behavioral interviews and technical interviews. Among Fortune 500 companies, behavior-based interviewing techniques now dominate as the preferred selection methodology. However, the most common practice is to conduct one-on-one behavioral interviews. In the companies that do encourage or even mandate team behavioral interviews, the interviewers typically ask the behavioral questions in such a choreographed manner that the so-called team interview turns out to be no more than a series of brief one-on-one interviews all conducted at the same venue. The Partnering Interview, on the other hand, provides an innovative approach for determining the breadth and depth of a job candidate's partnering competencies. Partnering with colleagues to conduct both a Partnering Interview and a structured behavioral interview provides a substantive advantage over conducting only one-on-one behavioral interviews; simply put, a Partnering Interview models partnering as "how things are done around here." Later in this chapter are examples of the kinds of questions to ask during a Partnering Interview, and a process for evaluating a candidate's Partnering Intelligence as an additional basis for making a sound selection decision.

A REFRESHER ON COMPETENCIES

Since the introduction over twenty years ago of job competence assessment (JCA) as a behaviorally anchored methodology for selection and development, various definitions of a competency and diverse kinds of competency models have emerged. *JCA* is a generic term describing an empirical methodology for isolating the historical characteristics of outstanding performance in a given job or role. JCA grew out of long-term research that found that certain traditional job selection criteria such as curriculum studied, alma mater, and grade point average are unreliable in predicting everyday performance on the job. Job competence assessment is founded on the premise that the best indicator of future performance is past performance under similar circumstances. Indeed, we are all creatures of habit.

In its "academically rigorous" form, JCA involves controlled interviews of both outstanding performers and average performers in the targeted job or role. Certified interviewers probe for detail around behavior in a series of specific situations known as "critical incidents." Note, however, that if an organization wants future performance to be substantively different from past performance, then some of the data that emerge from these interviews may oppose desired sets of behaviors going forward. In its rigorous form, JCA can take months and cost a bundle. Few organizations want to spend that much time and money for the incremental "validity" that comes with a rigorous approach. Other approaches have proven effective for creating a reliable, practicable competency model.

The branches of competency-based selection and development are both varied and numerous. And devotees of each throw rocks at each other with comparable abandon. The authors have personally worked with client companies whose competency models have comprised as few as a dozen competencies (or less), as well as with others whose competency models have totaled as many as three hundred (yes, three hundred). We have seen the same competency descriptor— for example, communication—defined in some models as a discrete competency, and in other models as a cluster encompassing as many as a half-dozen individual "communication competencies" (e.g., listening, oral presentations, writing, giving feedback, and so on). We have seen competency models in which a particular competency—for example, leadership—is defined by as few as two or three tightly written one-line behavioral indicators, and we have come across other models in which the specific behavioral indicators for leadership number as many as fifteen or sixteen, with many of the behavioral indicators in fact consisting of a mixture of several different behaviors. Thus, before introducing the partnering competencies vital to building and sustaining a partnering organization, it is important to set the stage by clearly defining the authors' understanding of competencies.

We define *competency* as a characteristic of an individual that can be shown to predict outstanding performance in a job. In short, competencies are the traits, knowledge, skills, and abilities that enable the behaviors essential to producing the principal outputs of a job. Accurate self-assessment is an example of a competency; keyboarding (née touch-typing) is not. Initiative is a competency; knowing how to jazz up a slide presentation by inserting a flapping blue butterfly is not. Neither keyboarding nor jazzing up a slide presentation will drive outstanding performance. In certain organizations, however, accurate self-assessment and initiative can be crucial to delivering superior results. The main purpose of competencies is thus to paint a detailed picture of what outstanding performance looks like in terms that can be openly—and ideally, rationally—debated with empirical data.

The picture of success must be painted in terms of observable behaviors that apply specifically to a particular job, in a particular unit, in a particular organization. In behavioral terms, for example, the competency teamwork for a reactor engineering supervisor in a nuclear power plant will look different from that of a financial analyst in an insurance firm. In both cases, however, a selecting leader would develop a job profile to help define the future-focused traits, knowledge, skills, and abilities needed to carry out the organization's strategic goals (see the section "The Partnering Paradox in Job Design" in Chapter 5). Competencies can enable the accomplishment of enterprise objectives such as the following:

- Set behavioral norms that will foster desired cultural changes

- Lay the groundwork for a new kind of employer–employee compact

- Increase the effectiveness of a selection process

- Raise performance standards

- Improve alignment of individual behaviors with strategic direction

- Serve as a set of criteria for measuring performance and career growth

- Enable innovative pay programs such as broadbanding and pay for knowledge

- Focus training and development plans on the most critical areas of need

- Foster a learning organization

In summary, competencies can serve as the centerpiece of an integrated human performance system.

An organization's competencies are most directly derived both from its strategic framework and from the corresponding business processes, both core and enabling. An organization's purpose drives its business processes, and its purpose and its processes together define its core competencies, the subset of the myriad competencies that define how the enterprise would like to be viewed by customers, employees, and owners. Usually, twelve to fifteen competencies serve as an adequate means of making sound selections and as the basis for an empirically based human performance and development system.

COMPETENCIES AND BEHAVIORAL INDICATORS

Competencies must be both generally defined and specifically described in behavioral terms. A behavioral indicator is an observable behavior that indicates the presence of the particular competency. It is this type of indicator for which a selecting manager will probe in conducting a behavioral interview of a candidate. The more behavioral indicators that surface during the interview, the greater the likelihood that the candidate is strong in a particular competency. For example, the competency communication can be defined as listening effectively and transmitting information accurately and understandably. Behavioral indicators for communication might include writing clearly, logically, and to the point; using simple examples, illustrations, or analogies to explain complex concepts; and so on. Table 5 illustrates other examples of generic competencies with behavioral indicators.

Further, sample behavioral inquiries must be designed to help interviewers probe for detailed evidence of the competencies required for a job. The presence of a particular competency in an individual—and the degree to which that competency is characteristic of the person—is evidenced by an interrelated set of behavioral indicators: what the person has said and has done. Not what he or she might say and do, could say and do, would say and do, or ought to say and do. Validity comes only from considering what he or she has in fact said, and has in fact done—that is, empirical behavioral data. Sample questions are targeted at uncovering empirical data on the degree to which a candidate has demonstrated the behaviors critical to achieving

TABLE 5
Examples of Generic Competencies with Behavioral Indicators

Accountability: *accepting responsibility for personal actions, results, and costs*
- Make personal sacrifices to meet challenging goals, schedules, or budgets
- Express a concern for doing things better and producing quality work
- Acknowledge responsibility for failures and mistakes

Drive to Win: *hustling to find and leverage opportunities to close a sale*
- Maintain an aggressive cold-call schedule at all times, regardless of frustrations
- Find opportunities to provide additional products and services to customers
- Look across boundaries to grow the business

Technical Expertise: *demonstrating up-to-date knowledge of pertinent technical fields*
- Find practical applications for new technology on the job
- Demonstrate curiosity and enthusiasm for technical aspects of the job
- Ask for and take on more challenging technical work

the principal accountabilities of a specific job. Table 6 provides examples of sample behavioral interview lead inquiries and probing follow-up questions; refer back to Table 5 for specific behavioral indicators.

Selecting leaders must also develop their own targeted leads that focus on specific situations and special circumstances someone in the position must face. The same set of targeted questions can then be used in all candidate interviews for a position.

The central challenge in building a competency model, or menu, is to create the right mix of both core organizational competencies and job-specific competencies, while keeping the list short—no more than twelve to fifteen. Remember, a competency model is not intended to list each and every competency that might ever apply to a specific job, but rather to identify the fewest number of competencies that make the biggest difference in performance when comparing the

TABLE 6
Examples of Behavioral Interview Lead Inquiries and Probing Follow-up Questions

For Accountability:
Talk about an instance when you made a personal sacrifice to get the job done.
- How did you feel about having to make the personal sacrifice?
- What was it that drove you to make the personal sacrifice?
- How did you feel about the results you achieved?

For Drive to Win:
Tell me about a time when you turned a cold call into a big piece of business.
- How did you respond to prospect objections?
- What was the reason you succeeded in closing this sale?
- What kind of relationship have you built with that customer?

For Technical Expertise:
Give an example of how you have applied a new technology on the job.
- What steps did you specifically take to bring in the new technology?
- Which of your technical strengths worked for you especially well in this situation?
- What obstacles did you encounter in introducing the new technology?

track records of outstanding performers with the results of average performers. Purpose drives the core competencies, the characteristics that are most vital in shaping organization culture going forward, and against which everyone in the organization must be assessed. Business processes drive job-specific competencies. Often, organizations will build supplemental technical competency menus for critical functions or roles—for example, a nuclear engineering competency model for a nuclear power plant or a deal originator competency model for a financial services firm. Organizations rarely build competency menus for all levels or functions.

In preparing a job profile that documents the relevant competencies for a specific position, it is critical that selecting leaders focus only on the principal accountabilities of a position going forward, rather than on any person who might currently hold the position. The selecting leader describes each competency in the context of the position, weights each relative to the others, and gets management approval. The job profile then becomes the standard for selecting the best-qualified candidate.

PARTNERING COMPETENCIES

People partner. If you want to build a partnering organization, you must hire, grow, and keep either people who are already smart partners or people who are capable of rapidly—and cost-effectively—becoming smart partners. The preliminary steps discussed in Chapter 5 include

- Establishing a strategic framework that espouses the values of smart partnering

- Implementing a systematic partnering process such as smart partnering

- Reshaping the organization as a partnering network to enable connections among people

Yet none of these necessary steps for building a partnering organization mean much unless the people behave as smart partners, internally and externally, day in and day out. When the people of a company are behaving as smart partners every day, then partnering will have become "how things are done around here." The organization will have created a partnering culture.

Generic core competencies such as accountability and specific technical competencies such as negotiation skills will of course continue to be necessary for successful job performance, but they will no longer be sufficient for sustaining success in the Dual Age of Information and Connections. To build a partnering organization, twenty-first-century leaders will have to incorporate a set of partnering competencies into the mix of selection and development criteria. Some organizations have already begun to include partnering-related competencies as elements in their competency models. For example, many companies we have worked with have included win-win negotiation as a specific core organizational competency. All we are suggesting is that these kinds of partnering-related competencies be filled out with some or all of the partnering competencies derived from the Six Partnering Attributes.

Based on statistical analysis of the results of thousands of Partnering Quotient (PQ) Assessments we have administered over the past five years and on anecdotal evidence we have gathered in working with client companies over the last twenty, we have put together a suite of six partnering competencies (each derived from one of the Six Partnering Attributes) and a comprehensive set of behavioral indicators for each of the partnering competencies. For simplicity, we have designated the six partnering competencies by the same names.

1. **Self-Disclosure and Feedback:** *promoting the frequent, open, mutual exchange of business information, points of view, and performance feedback*

   Self-Disclosure and Feedback is the cornerstone of every successful partnership. Demonstrating the behaviors associated with this competency is the first step in becoming a smart partner, a more effective partner. Self-disclosure offers the first opportunity to build trust in a partnership. The more information you reveal about yourself to your partners, the more your partners will trust you, and the more readily they will reveal information to you. The more potential partners know about your needs, the greater the chance that they can help figure out a way you can get those needs met. The ability to give partners feedback is also crucial to sustaining a successful partnership. If you cannot provide feedback to your partners on their behavior, especially in conflict situations, you must suppress your feelings, an action that will inevitably lead to resentment, a breakdown in communication, and counterproductive behavior on your part. Also, how you receive feedback from your partners will determine to a great degree the environment you create for future feedback you must give to your partners. If you expect your partners to receive and view your feedback as a gift, you must likewise encourage and accept their feedback as a gift.

2. **Win-Win Orientation:** *pursuing objectives, solving problems, and resolving conflicts in a collaborative manner that consistently creates winners all around*

Creating win-win outcomes is an overriding objective in any successful partnership. Partnerships that produce losers are destined to fail, usually sooner rather than later. For a partnership to thrive and grow, each partner must feel like a winner, and each partner must believe that he or she has personally contributed to making the other partners also feel like winners. Having a win-win orientation means using problem-solving and conflict resolution strategies that solve problems and resolve issues in a manner in which everyone feels like they win. When you and your partner have the same, or similar, objectives, creating a win-win outcome is a breeze. But if you and your partner have different needs, perhaps not mutually compatible, you will have to use win-win strategies to ensure that all involved get their needs met. Whatever your preferred style for solving problems and resolving conflicts, you can learn more effective strategies to ensure win-win outcomes. Remember, partnerships are formed to fulfill specific needs. How we get these needs met becomes part of the system that creates and sustains productive partnerships.

3. **Ability to Trust:** *giving trust unreservedly, honoring one's commitments, and acting in a manner that builds one's personal credibility*

Of all the dynamics involved in smart partnering, trust is the single most crucial. Trust is the system of reliable responses that binds together social orders. It can be thought of as the climate of a relationship, and it is shaped by what you and your partner say or do not say, or do or do not do, within the context of the partnership. If you violate a norm or expectation you have established, or when you act arbitrarily or beyond the limits of your usual behavior patterns, whether intentionally or accidentally, you can confuse and upset others. Trust is created when mutual expectations are satisfied not just once, or in isolated instances, but consistently, under a variety of circumstances. Breeches of trust can shake a partnership to its foundation and require enormous amounts of time, energy, focus, and often money to repair. Trust is not owed by one partner to another, but rather must be created, nurtured, and sustained over time through repeated personal interactions. Trust is both an input to and an output of successful partnerships.

4. **Future Orientation:** *creating a clear vision of the future, committing oneself to that vision, and building the confidence of others in that vision*

Whenever you encounter a new situation or meet new people, you do so with a set of attitudes and expectations. If you have a past orientation, you tend to force fit your past experiences into a new situation. If you have a future orientation, you are more likely to see the possibilities inherent in a new situation and approach it openly with good faith and hope. Typically, you enter a new partnership mostly with, sometimes only with, past information about your prospective partner—what you think you know about the prospective partner or what you have heard secondhand about the person. As you build trust with your partner, you become more confident in planning together for the future. Your mutual vision for the partnership serves as the future orientation for your collaborative efforts, the energy that propels the partnership forward. While you and your partner are working together to achieve your partnership goals, the vision you jointly established serves both as a guiding star to ensure that you stay on course and as a benchmark against which to measure progress.

5. **Comfort with Change:** *stepping out of one's own comfort zone, looking for new opportunities in marketplace changes, and encouraging others to embrace change*

By their very nature, partnerships involve change. In the broadest sense, the perceived need to change—to do something different— is one of the most fundamental reasons for creating a partnership. Just like individuals, organizations periodically need change and renewal. The act of reaching out to form a new partnership in and of itself will disrupt the status quo of an organization and force change, ready or not. Each of us responds to the reality of these kinds of changes in a different way. Some battle to minimize change and its effects on them, while others enthusiastically embrace, and often create, change. Particularly, imposed change affects our thoughts, feelings, and actions, often producing a knee-jerk response. The key to coping with our changing relationships and marketplaces is to remember that although we cannot always control change, we can control how we respond to it. In many instances, partnerships fail because the partners do not have adequate skills for, or put too little time into, building the relationship component of the partnership, an activity that can involve a great degree of personal change. By saying, "I'm fine the way I am; it is my partner who needs to change," a partner walks away from his or her responsibility to embrace personal change.

6. **Comfort with Interdependence:** *championing interreliance, relying on others for key results, and fostering interpersonal connections and informal networks*

We do not use the word *interdependence* much in Western cultures. We champion individuals and have built a culture on hard work and self-reliance. But, whereas the twentieth-century marketplace demanded independence and competition, the twentieth-first-century marketplace will require interdependence. With expanding technology and quickly shifting demands for complex goods and services, organizations are finding that they cannot by themselves satisfy all their customers' wants and needs. Just as people adopt predominantly independent or interdependent attitudes in their partnerships, businesses foster a workplace culture in which either independence or interdependence dominates. Interdependence obliges each member of a partnership to give up some control, and giving up control requires a high level of trust in other partners. Interdependence is a tall order, but when organizational leaders value interdependence and act interdependently, they create a work environment that encourages involvement. With increased interaction, people develop a sense that "we're all in this together," and information flows freely, trust is strengthened, and win-win outcomes become the only acceptable results.

Table 7 provides a sampling of the behavioral indicators accompanying each of the six partnering competencies. Part 4 of the partnering organization case study, continued from Chapter 5, illustrates how competencies can help drive a strategic organizational transformation by creating a partnering culture.

PARTNERING INTERVIEW

A Partnering Interview is a structured behavioral interview that assesses a candidate's strengths as a smart partner. This collaborative methodology uses tailored questions to elicit concrete examples of a candidate's past experience and behavior in situations similar to those of the open position. This empirical methodology allows a hiring manager to assess a candidate's qualifications objectively against the set of partnering competencies required for success. In a Partnering Interview, three to five interviewers, including the hiring manager, share responsibility for asking questions, probing, and taking notes. Conducting a Partnering Interview as a team provides multiple perspectives on a candidate's competencies, distributes responsibility for

TABLE 7
Partnering Competencies with Sample Behavioral Indicators

Self-Disclosure and Feedback: *promoting the frequent, open, mutual exchange of business information, points of view, and performance feedback*
- Share information with all partners fully, accurately, and promptly
- Give partners timely, fact-based coaching to help them perform better
- Deliver difficult messages in a manner that maintains positive relations with partner

Win-Win Orientation: *pursuing objectives, solving problems, and resolving conflicts in a collaborative manner that consistently creates winners all around*
- Seek out information needed to determine partner requirements
- Consider a wide spectrum of viewpoints on critical issues and concerns
- Resolve differences by seeking mutually beneficial solutions

Ability to Trust: *giving trust unreservedly, honoring one's commitments, and acting in a manner that builds one's personal credibility*
- Spend informal time with partners to discover their hidden wants and needs
- Tell the truth straightforwardly and with concern for partner's situation
- Accept responsibility for actions taken and outcomes produced

Future Orientation: *creating a clear vision of the future, committing oneself to that vision, and building the confidence of others in that vision*
- Create strategies to enable the achievement of both short-term and long-term goals
- Stay energized about the vision regardless of disappointment or failure
- Encourage prudent risk taking and entrepreneurial approaches

Comfort with Change: *stepping out of one's own comfort zone, looking for new opportunities in marketplace changes, and encouraging others to embrace change*
- Solicit unusual or nontraditional points of view
- Question established ways of doing things when choosing a course of action
- Move quickly in response to changes in direction, products, and market segments

Comfort with Interdependence: *championing interreliance, relying on others for key results, and fostering interpersonal connections and informal networks*
- Work across boundaries to achieve business goals and objectives
- Encourage partners to take initiative and to make their own decisions
- Help partners acquire information, training, and other necessary resources

PARTNERING ORGANIZATION CASE STUDY: CREATING A WORLD-CLASS SUPPLY-CHAIN ORGANIZATION

Part 4: Partnering Competencies

Once the structure team defined the roles of supply managers and supply service representatives, it became apparent that the jobs called for different, higher-level skills—a new set of *competencies.* The supply management team approach led to establishing a set of twelve key supply management competencies for the new positions. These competencies are in fact comparable to those of sales managers and customer service representatives.

The Supply Management Competency Model, designed to function as the DNA of the strategic framework of the reconfigured procurement function, includes three competency categories as outlined below. Four competencies—*comfort with change, comfort with interdependence, drive to cut costs,* and *negotiation skills*—were designated core competencies. They are considered the absolute baseline requirements for any hire because of their vital link to successful future performance of a supply management team. The selection team eliminated from further consideration any candidate who did not furnish multiple, varied behavioral examples demonstrating these four core competencies in high measure.

Partnering Competencies

- **Self-disclosure and feedback:** representing the company's needs straightforwardly and seeking to understand the needs of all stakeholders

- **Win-win orientation:** building collaboration among internal customers, vendors, and Finance and working to achieve group goals and outcomes

- *Comfort with change:* adjusting to how individuals, organizational units, and cultures function and react

- *Comfort with interdependence:* empowering people to achieve desirable, agreed-upon outcomes and trusting them to follow through

Individual Performance Competencies

- *Drive to cut costs:* aggressively persisting to drive down costs of purchased goods and services
- **Communication skills:** transmitting information accurately, understandably, and effectively
- **Analytical skills:** recognizing patterns in data, information, or events, drawing logical conclusions, and making recommendations for action
- **Problem solving and decision making:** taking a well-ordered approach to solving problems and acting confidently despite obstacles or resistance
- **Planning and organization skills:** anticipating future events and structuring resources and actions in a logical manner

Technical Competencies

- *Negotiation skills:* influencing others to get their agreement on terms for the purchase of goods and services
- **Vendor expertise:** demonstrating broad, in-depth knowledge of internal and external supply sources
- **Global commodity knowledge:** demonstrating detailed knowledge of worldwide markets for specified commodities

focused probes and focused listening, and requires less time for the overall interview process. The basic steps involved in preparing for and conducting structured behavioral interviews are well documented, and so we present only refresher points here. Figure 6 illustrates a general format for a team Partnering Interview.

For a team Partnering Interview to produce the empirical data needed to make a sound selection decision, every member of the interview team must be trained in the methodology. The most common comment we have received from our clients in this regard is that it is a whole lot harder than it looks. Without individual feedback on interviewing techniques from an experienced interviewer, a new

FIGURE 6
Partnering Interview Format (Sample)

The Partnering Interview consists of four parts: opening, obtaining information, providing information, and closing. Interviews can take from thirty to ninety minutes, depending on the position and preinterview investigation.

A. **Opening** (Hiring Manager)
   1. Welcome the candidate, establish rapport, and introduce other interviewers.
   2. Make sure the candidate is comfortable (chair, lighting, room temperature).
   3. Explain how the Partnering Interview will be conducted.
      a. Focus on the partnering competencies required for the position.
      b. Explain that you and other interviewers will be taking notes.
      c. Review basics of a behavioral interview (if new to candidate).
      d. Indicate that there will be time for questions at the end.
   4. Briefly describe the position, or show candidate the job description.

B. **Obtaining Information** (Partnering Interview Team)
   1. Use your interview plan: ask a broadbrush question . . . be quiet and listen . . . probe for detail . . . be quiet and listen . . . probe . . . listen . . . close the episode.
   2. Probe for more information based on the candidate's response.
   3. Gather sufficient examples to assess the candidate in one competency before moving to the next.
   4. Clarify remaining discrepancies, gaps, or questions from your review of the résumé.

C. **Providing Information** (Hiring Manager)
   1. Go into more detail about the position (discuss job description).
   2. Respond to candidate's questions about the position.

D. **Closing** (Hiring Manager)
   1. Give cues that the interview is nearing its end.
   2. Thank the candidate.
   3. Describe what happens next.
   4. Conclude with final rapport building.

interviewer is highly prone to lapse into a traditional interview protocol and style, resulting in such useless mindbenders as, "If you could be a tree, what kind of tree would you be?" At the end of this chapter we have summarized some commonsense tips on team behavioral interviewing. But remember: Tips are not a substitute for training.

The Partnering Interview Plan is a tool we've developed that interviewers can use prior to interviews to note critical questions to ask and also during interviews to ensure that they probe all relevant partnering competencies. The Partnering Interview Plan is structured with preplanned questions listed in a prescribed order and focuses on one competency at a time. An interviewer does not move on until satisfied that enough behavioral data have been gathered to evaluate the candidate on that competency. But a Partnering Interview Plan is also flexible, allowing any interviewer on the team to probe for additional information based on the candidate's responses and examples to validate information previously gathered about the candidate from other sources such as a résumé, internal references, or a screening interview. The plan also specifies roles for the Partnering Interview team including the following:

- Hiring manager:
  - ✓ Opens and closes the Partnering Interview
  - ✓ Describes the position and the partnering competencies
  - ✓ Asks questions related to the specific competencies

- Partnering Interview team member:
  - ✓ Asks questions and probes assigned competencies
  - ✓ Listens for examples of assigned competencies in response to questions about other competencies
  - ✓ Takes brief notes related to the candidate's responses

- Facilitator/timekeeper:
  - ✓ Keeps interview questions and probes focused on behavioral data
  - ✓ Monitors time overall and for each competency
  - ✓ Makes smooth transitions between competencies
  - ✓ Ensures that the team covers all the competencies before wrapping up

FIGURE 7
Partnering Interview Plan Extract (Sample)

Position/Title:	Candidate Name:
Hiring Manager:	____ Initial Interview ____ Follow-up Interview
Team Members and Facilitator:	
Interview Date & Time:	Interview Location:
Background:	

1. **Self-disclosure and feedback:** promoting the frequent, open, mutual exchange of business information, points of view, and performance feedback.

1.1 Give an example of when you raised an emotional issue with a subordinate or colleague.
1.2 Describe a time when you asked for feedback on a project you were working on.
1.3 Talk about a situation in which you gave someone else performance feedback.

Notes:

Figure 7 shows a sample one-page extract from a Partnering Interview Plan.

Part 5 of the continuing partnering organization case study illustrates how a Partnering Interview can help ensure the selection of the job candidates who demonstrate the partnering competencies at the highest levels. It also contains a note on "paying for partnering."

PARTNERING ORGANIZATION CASE STUDY: CREATING A WORLD-CLASS SUPPLY-CHAIN ORGANIZATION

Part 5: Partnering Interview

To ensure that every member of the new supply management team had the "right stuff" and to signal to employees and vendors alike that a strategic change was underway in the procurement function, the company decided to restaff the organization. They launched an aggressive search for highly qualified individuals to fill the positions with people who had the new set of competencies, starting with the top position, vice president of supply management. Candidates came from both inside and outside the company, with a distinctive variety of backgrounds in procurement and inventory management, finance, engineering, and manufacturing operations.

The company chose to use the Partnering Interview as its methodology for screening preliminary candidates, evaluating final candidates, and making selection decisions. Once the president and a team of senior leaders agreed on who would fill the position of vice president of supply management, the new VP immediately took a strong lead in the staffing process, partnering with Human Resources to involve managers from Sales, Marketing, Engineering, and Manufacturing in the Partnering Interview process.

A team of at least three interviewers conducted every interview, and most interview teams had four members. In each case, the hiring manager led the interview team, supported by at least one internal customer and a staffing professional from Human Resources. For the supply manager positions, an operations manager or a production foreman from one of the manufacturing plants was added as a fourth Partnering Interview team member. The same team conducted Partnering Interviews of all the candidates for a particular opening so that every selector heard from every candidate for that position. Secondhand information on competencies of candidates was prohibited. Employees who previously held purchasing positions were given primary consideration for the new jobs. They were given copies of the new job descriptions and the Supply Management Competency Model, and they received third-party training to prepare for the interview process.

At the conclusion of the staffing process over 60 percent of the incumbents in the existing procurement function were replaced. The new supply managers and supply service representatives were selected on the basis of both their partnering competencies and individual performance competencies, with a combination of strong technical skills, as well as proven expertise in negotiations and sales. Those individuals who were not placed elsewhere in the company received severance packages and outplacement support.

Note on "Paying for Partnering"

It was also apparent that by raising the bar for the type of people needed in the reconfigured organization, the company needed to build a new compensation system to attract, retain, and motivate skilled people. According to the new vice president of supply management, a major factor in ensuring the success of the staffing process was an innovative compensation strategy. Attracting candidates with the right mix of competencies (partnering, individual performance, and technical) required a flexible salary schedule that would pay for partnering on par with Sales and Marketing. The company introduced a "broadband" salary scale that could cover both the supply managers and the supply service representatives, with bands of pay that allowed for sensible differentiation on the bases of both the strategic magnitude of assigned commodities and the strategic importance of critical vendor relationships. Additionally, based on personal and supply management team achievements, supply managers would be eligible for incentives that could total as much as 1.75 months' salary, a performance incentive on par with their Sales and Marketing counterparts.

TIPS FOR CONDUCTING
TEAM PARTNERING INTERVIEWS

To close out this chapter we offer a list of commonsense tips for conducting effective team Partnering Interviews divided into four aspects—inquiry strategies, questioning techniques, questioning pitfalls, and what to probe.

1. **Inquiry Strategies**

   - The easiest way to get the truth is to make the candidate comfortable

   - Know what you are looking for, ask the right question . . . then listen

   - If the interview is the candidate's first behavioral interview, take the first five to ten minutes of the interview to train the candidate in how to respond

   - Give the candidate the chance to talk first about a few successes before asking for an example of something that did not go well

   - When the candidate cannot come up with an example within ten seconds, ask a different broadbrush question and come back to the first question later

   - Your most powerful tool as an interviewer is silence

2. **Questioning Techniques**

   - Frame questions in the past tense to signal that you want a factual response

   - Ask only one question at a time . . . then listen . . . probe . . . listen

   - Ask the candidate to headline a major story's beginning, middle, and end

   - To personalize a story, ask for the names of key players (unless the information is highly sensitive)

   - When the candidate uses "we," ask, "Who specifically did that?"

- To move a story along, ask, "What did you do next?" or, "What happened next?"

- If the candidate begins to give irrelevant details, say, as appropriate, "Let's get back to your main actions at that time," or, "Let's move on to another area."

- To uncover underlying logic, say, "Walk me step by step through . . ."

- To get under the hood for special accomplishments, ask, "How did you do that?"

- To nudge for more detail, try these four words: "Tell me more about . . ."

- To surface attribute competencies, ask, "What was going through your mind?"

- To bring an episode to a close, ask, "How did you feel about the outcome?"

3. Questioning Pitfalls

- Asking multiple questions at the same time

- Relying on questions that can be answered "yes" or "no"

- Repeating the same question when the candidate does not instantly respond

- Jumping in too soon when there is "dead air"

- Leading the candidate to the answer you want

- Permitting the candidate to continue to use "you" or "we" without clarifying the candidate's specific role

- Letting the candidate respond in the present tense or the subjunctive (would, could, should, ought, might) without pressing for a specific example of what he or she has actually done

- Allowing the candidate to talk in generalities without pushing for a specific example

- Working over a candidate when it's clear that the candidate is stuck in trying to respond to a particular question or probe

4. What to Probe

- Complex events involving many players
- Events that evoke strong emotion, positive or negative
- Anything out of the ordinary
- Frequent dodges such as "I can't exactly recall," "That was two years ago," "Well, there were a lot of people involved," or "We did it as a team"
- Repeated lapses into the use of "we" or "you"
- Inconsistencies in the narration of events
- Overreliance on a few stories—"crutch events"
- Generalizations, assertions, and inferences
- Adjectives and adverbs

Hiring Smart Partners

In this chapter we have talked about how companies must rethink the competencies they view as core to their organization's culture and their success. In the twenty-first century, smart partnering is emerging as one of the preeminent competencies needed for outstanding job performance. We have discussed the competencies that directly drive partnering behaviors. These partnering-enabling competencies must form the foundation of an organization's human performance system in the Dual Age of Information and Connections. Hiring people with these partnering competencies will accelerate the building of a partnering culture, and thus a partnering organization. We have shown what it takes to identify these partnering competencies and ensure their alignment with a strategic framework, the success of which hinges on smart partnering.

We have introduced the concept of a Partnering Interview. The Partnering Interview is a proprietary, innovative approach for determining the breadth and depth of a job candidate's partnering competencies. Partnering with colleagues to conduct both a Partnering Interview and a structured behavioral interview provides a substantive advantage over conducting only one-on-one behavioral interviews.

Simply put, a Partnering Interview models partnering as "how things are done around here." We have presented a protocol for a Partnering Interview, given examples of the kinds of questions to ask during the interview, and outlined a process for evaluating a candidate's Partnering Intelligence as an additional basis for making a sound selection decision. We have provided an extract of a Partnering Interview Plan, a tool that interviewers can use prior to interviews to note critical questions to ask and also during interviews to ensure that interviewers probe all relevant partnering competencies. A Partnering Interview Plan is both structured (it employs preplanned questions that focus on one competency at a time) and flexible (any interviewer can probe for additional information based on the candidate's responses and examples). Finally, we have furnished some commonsense tips with easy-to-follow suggestions for conducting team Partnering Interviews. In Chapter 7 we turn our attention from hiring smart partners to trying to keep them—and to make them even smarter.

7

Keeping and Growing Smart Partners

Any idea . . . that my visit would bolster the morale of these men was overshadowed by the effect the visit had on [me]. . . . Each man had a cheery word . . . [My] misgivings that these men would weaken under the hardships of their cramped position and the adverse weather . . . faded away into nothing.

—CHARLES BROWN MACDONALD, *COMPANY COMMANDER*

A large telecommunications company we work with is in trouble. While business appears to be growing at a steady rate, employee turnover has swelled considerably higher than the industry norm. As CEO, Paul is confused and concerned. He believes he has created a workplace environment that is both challenging and fun. He feels that wages are competitive and that company-provided incentives are both generous and attractive. As an example, he cites the Chairman's Award, a ten-day Mediterranean cruise given to top performers. Truly baffled by the high turnover rate, Paul wonders why the people in the office always seem frazzled and demotivated. When we reviewed with Paul the events of the past year, we recalled a vivid episode related to us by the marketing vice president, Cindy.

Partnering Culture

NO LEADER IS AN ISLAND—PAUL'S STORY

Paul had hired Cindy, a smart, experienced woman who is a master at marketing strategy, and given her the mission to build a marketing and sales platform for growing the business based on two fundamental strategies: incremental improvements in product design and delivery, and consistency in service. In fact, Cindy had surrounded herself with some of the "coolest" people in the industry, co-workers who not only understood technical trends in telecommunications, but, more important to their market, also had a handle on fashion trends. It seems that teens and twenty-somethings wouldn't want to be caught dead with an "ugly" mobile phone. These young people consider how a phone looks as important as its operation, its technical features, and the number of monthly minutes that come with a particular billing plan. Also fancying himself as a hip guy, for a fifty-something, Paul felt he had his finger on the pulse of the younger generation.

While checking out the latest wireless phone gadgets at a vendor conference, his eye caught a glittery purple phone he knew in his bones would fly off the shelves. Without consulting Cindy or any-one else on the executive team (such as the vice presidents of customer service, engineering, or finance), or anyone else on the marketing and sales team (such as the director of sales or retail store managers), on the spot Paul ordered five thousand of the purple phones. The vendor at the conference was so pleased with the order that he gave Paul the floor sample to take back to show his team.

Paul strutted into his next executive staff meeting like a victo-rious Roman emperor, holding the glittering object of his affection high above his head, proudly announcing that this purple phone would be the next hottest thing on the market. He could hear cash registers ringing, even as members of his team stood frozen in dis-belief. Just two weeks before Paul bought the five thousand purple phones, the marketing team had agreed on the styles and colors of the new phones they would be featuring in the spring promotion; the marketing team had hired an ad agency to start work on marketing collaterals, signed contracts with handset vendors, and booked media slots. Gently, Cindy tried to probe to determine the extent of the damage Paul had caused. When Paul proudly blurted out that he had captured the market on purple phones, Cindy and her executive team colleagues were dumbfounded.

As tactfully as they could, she and her colleagues expressed the concern that the executive team had already endorsed the product offerings for the spring promotion and that the promotion launch was well underway. Paul, sensing resistance to his plan and to his five thousand beloved purple phones, went into a rage. Berating the executive team for lack of inventiveness and insisting that he had found the Holy Grail and that they were too blind to see it, he ranted and raved for twenty minutes. Finally, the defeated execu-tive team agreed to include the purple phone in the spring promo—as if they had a choice.

The redoing of the ad plan was expensive enough, but what really hurt was how the team felt after Paul's public berating. The post–executive team meeting—with Paul not there—revealed why the employee turnover rate had grown so high. Angry and resentful, three executives had become so personally frustrated with Paul and his inconsistent management style that they were openly talking about leaving. However, to a member, not one of them would confront Paul. Rather, they would meet privately with each other, complain about Paul and his erratic behavior, then go back to their offices and sulk about him and the messes he created, all because he could never stick to plan.

This was not the first time Paul had ridden roughshod over his team and changed the direction of their plans. In fact, people had become used to Paul's constant interference in the planning of everyday events. It's not that Paul was a micromanager, because in fact he wasn't. But Paul would get an idea and pursue it with a vengeance, regardless of what others around him thought. Once, when he insisted on green rather than blue print in newspaper ads, his bullheadedness created such a stir that two people in market communications resigned. Of course, he was glad to see them go. After all, he had said, "They are being petty, and we don't need people like that around here."

None of what Paul did in and of itself was a horrible thing. Truly, he wanted to make things better and cared about the people in his business. But Paul forgot that he needed to do more than just buy the loyalty of his employees. He did not understand that how he treated them was just as important as what he paid them. In retrospect, how Paul handled the introduction of the purple phones to his staff could have made all the difference in the world. Paul made a decision in isolation and then, without consideration for what his team had already accomplished for the spring promotion, unleashed a new element that totally upset their launch plans.

When we spoke with Cindy and the executive team afterward, they were beyond angry. Cindy summed up their feelings: "Paul does these things to us all the time, and people are fed up with it. We plan a whole seasonal promotion, and then he waltzes in with a hare-brained idea. He expects us just to 'adapt.' No wonder we're losing staff. Who wants to work under these conditions?"

SMART LEADERS, SMART PARTNERS

In the emerging information and connection economy, interpersonal relationships act as transmission conduits, as connectors. Computers regularly send digital messages back and forth, but humans convert those bytes and bits into something of value: a new product, market, or service. That value grows exponentially when two or more people get together and in a creative blitz turn something ordinary into something extraordinary. The genius at work does not reside in any one person; it resides in a culture that enables people to do what they do.

People add value whether by serving customers, building or selling products, or running the business. When employees are treated as trusted partners in an enterprise, they are freed up to pool their collective creative energies for the benefit of the business as a whole. Smart partners enable robust creativity by building an organization culture that encourages as many connections as possible. More connections produce more good ideas; more good ideas result in more great ideas; and more great ideas deliver extraordinary innovation. Paradoxically, an abundance view of the world stimulates creativity, and creativity in turn fuels abundance.

In short, smart partners drive creativity by increasing the frequency, the frankness, and the fruitfulness of interpersonal connections, dialogue, and collaboration. An organization's leaders can take three steps to keep and grow smart partners:

- Build loyalty and a sense of duty

- Coach people to grow informal communication networks (pathways)

- Strengthen relationship skills: (1) the diversity management skills of leaders and (2) the partnering skills of employees

Leaders in Paul's position, or leaders who don't want to end up in Paul's position, would profit from understanding the concrete ways in which they can implement this three-pronged approach for keeping and growing smart partners. Growing loyalty is no longer just an option, and top managers must understand that they contribute greatly to their organization's culture. Informal networks serve as the hidden pathways over which information, ideas, and resources can continue to be exchanged in an elusive, fast-moving marketplace. Inbreeding of ideas leads to groupthink and the risk of missing the obvious. Leaders are required to manage a new kind of diversity, and employees require partnering skills to get others not only to tolerate such diversity, but also to cherish it as the fuel of creativity. Together, these three key action steps will help you keep and grow the people who make your business a success.

We begin this chapter by addressing the first two: building loyalty and a sense of duty, and coaching people on how to grow informal communication networks. Later we discuss strengthening leaders' relationship skills. The partnering skills of employees, as informed by a thorough understanding of the Six Partnering Attributes, are covered in more detail in Chapters 8–10.

LOYALTY AND A SENSE OF DUTY

Money doesn't guarantee loyalty, though in some cases it can serve as a sizeable down payment. Granting titles and positions is a game that has played itself out in most industries. People know their value and the value they create, and the smart ones move on when they feel they are not being fairly compensated. And when they move on, they take their knowledge—not only their technical expertise, but your business strategies, tactics, strengths, weaknesses, and customer lists— with them as well. A promising future is not what awaits executives who cannot build loyalty among their staff. If fact, once people feel they are earning the money they deserve, they begin to search for something more significant to satisfy an inner craving for fulfillment. Paradoxically, loyalty does not have to cost you much, or even any- thing (beyond a competitive pay and benefits package), but disloyalty can cost you a lot, or even everything.

Smart executives know how to transform workers from clock- punching employees into smart partners by encouraging and enabling them to forge the types of relationships that foster loyalty. Wise leaders do this by understanding and aligning organizational values with personal values, by recognizing the achievements of their people, and by transforming the employment relationship into a true partnership focused on the success of the enterprise. Everyone wants to feel valued for their intelligence, contributions, follow-through, and successes. People want to feel part of something greater than themselves. As you read in Chapter 5, a compelling strategic framework announces the inspiring intentions of an organization's leaders and acts as a beacon to attract smart partners who resonate with the organization's vision, values, ethical standards, and strategic directions. As you read in Chapter 6, the ability to identify and hire the people with the right partnering competencies ensures that an enterprise has the basic relationship skills required for building a Powerhouse Partner. Now is the time to build loyalty, a sense of duty and commitment to the organization. Hiring smart partners is one thing; keeping them and growing their partnering skills is an entirely different endeavor.

Equip Employees with the Right Tools and Training

We recently reviewed a documentary detailing how the U.S. military is using information to fight the war on terrorism. In Iraq and Afghanistan, the military's traditional chain of command has been enhanced with a network of information-gathering and information-disseminating tools. On the front line of twenty-first-century warfare, the antenna has replaced the cavalry sword as the symbol of advancing troops. Predator drones scan and photograph battlefields, every move is perfectly executed using the Global Positioning System, and many soldiers receive up-to-the-minute intel on PDAs.

Every business can learn two things from the military's new approach to battle. First, it's encouraging to see an institution as old and seemingly tradition bound as the American military fully embracing change. Second, and more significant, the military has clearly done more than invest in cool gadgets. For all these new toys to work, the armed forces—all of them—had to invest in the people who use them. How soldiers, sailors, airmen, and marines collect, manage, and apply this information is as important as what information they are managing.

Giving people the right technical tools and training is only part of the equation. Employees must also know how to build the relationships that drive trust among other employees, their customers, and their partners. The armed forces establish the relationship of trust because of the critical nature of operations on the battlefield. Soldiers must be able to trust each other as if their lives depended on it, because they do. Businesses are not that different. Sales in the field must depend on Manufacturing to deliver what was promised; Customer Service must work with the customer to deliver ongoing satisfaction. Everyone depends on each other for information and follow-through if the end result is to be winning and keeping customers.

Building and maintaining loyalty among officers (think management) and enlisted members (think employees) is an area in which the military has most businesses beat. We tend to think of the armed forces in terms of a chain of command, of a rigid hierarchy; but what we don't think about is how thoroughly the military takes care of its people. The army, air force, navy, and marine corps all shower their people with training and support because the leaders know that when you take care of people, they take care of you.

Knowing how to build loyalty is emerging as a rediscovered art. During the past several decades, short-term incentives drove business decisions, decimating employee loyalty. The hard lesson that many companies have learned, however, is that losing even one key employee to the competition can wreak havoc on a business's strategies, proprietary information, and customer lists. Moreover, employees who have defected often return to poach additional talent, and the organization suffers further harm. Remember when Novell acquired WordPerfect Corporation for $1.25 billion, then tried to ram its uptight culture down the throats of the laid-back WordPerfect management team? Remember how the WordPerfect team abandoned ship in droves, how WordPerfect product development stagnated, and how sales collapsed? Do you remember how many of that WordPerfect team were scooped up by that other big software company? Eventually throwing in the towel, Novell unloaded WordPerfect for $250 million, a book loss of a cool $1 billion. And you still think loyalty is just something for the folks in Human Resources to worry about?

Think about the people to whom you've been loyal. What was it about them that fostered your loyalty? Not surprisingly, different people are loyal for different reasons, and reasons for loyalty reside in part in our psychological makeup as human beings. We offer here two case studies in building loyalty: first Malcolm, then Sarah.

Building a culture that values loyalty is a key leadership responsibility. And since people are motivated to be loyal for different reasons, understanding loyalty motivators and incorporating them into your culture is critical. Building loyalty in your organization requires a holistic approach. It's up to leadership, not Human Resources. But if you embrace loyalty, loyalty will embrace you.

BUILDING LOYALTY THROUGH PROFESSIONAL DEVELOPMENT—MALCOLM'S STORY

Malcolm, a product engineer at a Minnesota silicon chip manufacturer, was good at his job, but he often felt he was being treated unjustly. He felt that he was being held back and not given any opportunity to demonstrate his leadership abilities. One day Malcolm told Allen, the division director, that he dreamed of leading a team of people to develop a new process that Malcolm believed would improve safety and reduce production time. The company's product, nearly microscopic silicon chips, are fragile, and the manufacturing process requires close-up work that even with safety glasses presents a hazard to the eyes, both from flying debris and general eye strain.

Malcolm's idea was to build magnifying canopies over the assembly site. These canopies would give assemblers a better view of their work and better protect them from flying debris. Allen was skeptical: Malcolm's idea would require a complete rethinking of how they approached the work. Nevertheless, Allen unleashed Malcolm's creativity and supported his every effort. At first, Malcolm was beset with a series of technical setbacks—even though his idea seemed like an elegant solution, getting the right combination of optics and protection was difficult. At one point the project looked doomed. However, Allen never wavered in his support. Eventually, Malcolm and his team had a breakthrough, earning Malcolm a promotion. He is now a regional manager for the division and an extremely loyal employee who is willing to pay back Allen's support tenfold.

"When Allen recognized my desire to improve the situation and supported and stuck with me, I felt like an important contributor to our business's success," says Malcolm. "All the money in the world couldn't change how I feel toward Allen and my company."

What did Allen do to build Malcolm's loyalty? First, he took a personal interest in Malcolm and his future. He listened to Malcolm and didn't dismiss Malcolm's complaint as mere whining. Allen realized that here was an employee who wanted to do more and he acted on that. Then, once the project was underway, Allen never wavered in his support. Though there were ups and downs in the project, Allen publicly took ownership along with Malcolm. He was willing to pin his success on his employee's success.

Businesses don't need to build loyalty just for the sake of building loyalty. Capturing the hearts and minds of your most important asset makes bottom-line sense. Loyal employees are more productive than employees who just don't care. Loyal employees are quick to offer ideas and suggestions for improvements. They act as a catalyst for positive energy within the culture. Loyal employees are more likely to defend and support management decisions than be critical and negative about them. Loyal employees will adapt to change quicker and provide less resistance.

Behaviors of loyal employees are contagious, and they tend to spread enthusiasm to customers, resulting in higher levels of customer care. If you don't like your employer, you probably don't care how you treat its customers. After all, you're just putting in time to collect a paycheck. However, if you do care about your organization, your colleagues, and your job, you'll care about customers and give them a high quality of service. You not only retain customers, you also grow your customer base because of your good reputation, thus growing profits. Employee loyalty translates into customer loyalty, producing a positive growth in the bottom line.

Leaders can begin to shape a partnering culture and build employee loyalty by taking the following actions:

BUILDING LOYALTY THROUGH PERSONAL DEVELOPMENT—SARAH'S STORY

Sarah was a midlevel manager in a bank. She loved her job. It provided her with a high level of professional satisfaction and personal development. However, she often felt torn between her vocation and the passion for her avocation, the ecological health of the barrier islands that lie off the coast of North Carolina. The past decade had seen an increase in vacation homes built on the islands and a decrease in the natural vegetation and wildlife that grows and thrives there. Over the past several years several tropical storms had hit the islands and eroded the beaches, causing even more extensive damage to the habitat.

Her boss, Ella, knew of Sarah's love for the barrier islands and that every year Sarah spent her summer vacation doing community service work on the islands, such as picking up trash, marking protected turtle and bird nesting areas, and replanting beach vegetation. Sarah even started a fund to help rebuild one of the beaches after a tropical storm grazed the state. Ella also knew that they were trying to build community banking relationships within the state and that people in that area had a choice of regionally located banks.

Ella introduced Sarah to Tom, the bank's vice president of community services. Sarah shared with Tom her passion about the barrier islands. Tom had an idea. What if the bank established a fund to support the rehabilitation of the barrier islands in the eastern parts of the three states that shared these island habitats? He also suggested that Sarah be given some time to coordinate volunteers from the bank to work on beach restoration projects during their free time. Sarah was overjoyed . . . literally speechless. She had never imagined that her employer would take such an interest, much less encourage her to pursue her passion.

Over the years, the bank has sponsored several restoration projects and has won the hearts of many people within the three-state area. Sarah has noticed an increase in the growth of sea oats, birds, and other wildlife that populate the habitat, while the bank has witnessed an increase in the number of customers.

What did Ella and Tom do to build Sarah's loyalty? Ella recognized a passion in Sarah that, while not totally focused on business, fit into the larger corporate picture. Tom quickly connected Sarah's passion with the mission of the bank's community service division. He understood that he had a resource both for fostering growth for the bank and for doing good in the community. He worked with Sarah to help her follow her passion while he also was able to achieve his goal of community service. Sarah was able to connect her passion with her vocation and is firmly committed to making sure her employer gets the very best she has to offer. From what we hear, that's been quite a bit. This situation has had a true win-win outcome for everyone involved.

- *Sharing an organizational vision that connects with employees' souls.* Business is about more than making money. Provide people with a greater purpose than just money and you will be surprised at how hard they will work for you.

- *Creating an environment of open and candid communication.* Closed marketplaces eventually collapse. Forums for the exchange of ideas and opinions operate the same way. Embrace freedom of expression and drive out every remnant of fear. Nothing kills creativity, innovation, and honesty quicker than fear. Fear is a mind killer. Fear is the mother of groupthink.

- *Recognizing that trust is a must.* Only one lapse of judgment can destroy a lifetime of building trust, and without trust there can be no loyalty. Guard trust as you would guard proprietary information . . . it's actually more valuable.

- *Generating opportunities for collaboration.* When people have the opportunity to participate in creating the work they execute, they feel as if they are a part of something bigger. Make collaboration an essential part of your business culture.

- *Offering hope.* Hope is one of the greatest human motivators and builders of loyalty. Every great movement, whether social, religious, or political, has offered participants hope. Be optimistic, and above all communicate. People can't believe in you if you don't articulate the vision.

- *Inspiring a duty to teamwork.* Encourage, cajole, do whatever you must to ensure that people work well together. Make sure that your compensation and reward structure reflects your desire for teamwork by finding a way to compensate the individual contributors and teamwork fairly.

Building a Sense of Duty Among Employees

Your employees are partners in the business. If you invest energy in your relationships with employees and work to promote their loyalty, they in turn will provide added value. If you do not invest in employees, ignore them, or abuse them, the opposite will occur. They will take advantage of you and leave you at the first opportunity, taking business knowledge with them and perhaps even try to diminish the company's reputation.

Being a business where people want to work is an important asset and growth strategy for many businesses. GMAC-RFC has an internal human resource campaign that includes posters of their employees. Under the picture are these words: "Human . . . Capital . . . In That Order." The message is that their business offers two products. The first is the human intelligence, knowledge, and relationships needed to make a deal. The second is the capital to fund a deal. But the stress is on people. They stress their ability to partner with customers, suppliers, and investors to create a win-win outcome, and they accomplish this not so much through financial capital, but through human beings. Anyone who has done business with GMAC-RFC knows that they value building trust and making sure deals are mutually beneficial. Working through issues until mutual satisfaction is achieved is a hallmark of their business and an important business strategy for their future.

Steele Alphin, chief people officer for Bank of America, talking about his partnership with Exult, a human resources partner, put it this way:

> We quickly realized an important truth about today's business environment: teamwork isn't always enough. The future of business is partnering. Team members share a common goal, but people working in partnership also share a common sense of duty. Partners take full responsibility for each other's success. As a result, the level of commitment is deeper, and the potential for reward is far greater.

When you have team members who take care of each other, look out for each other, protect each other, and make sure each member succeeds, you have a partnering culture that inspires success. In reality, few of those types of cultures exist in the business world today.

COACHING AND MENTORING TO BUILD INFORMAL COMMUNICATION NETWORKS

Successful cultures make sure that employees are given opportunities both to grow their talents and to cultivate organizational connections. One of the most successful techniques for accomplishing both aims is through a coaching and mentoring program. Connecting employees—especially those with high potential within your organization—with executive coaches helps to broaden and hone those relationships, connects people within the organization, and fosters the exchange of knowledge, information, and resources. The ability to influence others informally across an organization's structure has become increasingly important in today's flatter organizations. Leaders can maximize the human potential of a workforce by placing a high priority on mentoring and developing others. Great leaders understand the value of coaching.

Coaching isn't a one-way street, where leaders have all the answers, but rather a partnership in which both parties share ownership and responsibility. Wise leaders promote coaching and mentoring strategies that forge partnerships by engaging people, fostering collaboration, building strong and effective relationships, managing conflict, opening communication, and inspiring trust. Establishing a coaching and mentoring program to accelerate the cultivation of informal communication networks is an important step in creating a Powerhouse Partner. Such programs provide an opportunity for leaders to role-model the expected behaviors and attitudes they expect in the culture in a highly visible manner.

What exactly is coaching? Coaching is a partnership in which two individuals work together for mutual professional growth. The coach has experience and knowledge in the business that the employee wants to develop and provides input, feedback, and guidelines. Employees offer personal insights into the organization, giving the coach a grounded perspective and up-to-date information about the organization he or she may not otherwise receive. This feedback provides the opportunity for leader coaches to improve their coaching and mentoring skills and to receive feedback from those they coach. In addition to offering a channel to pass information from the top down, this invaluable network allows executives to receive information from the bottom up, from those they can trust. Coaching and mentoring can help boost an organization's efforts to become a partnering organization in a variety of ways, including

- Developing professional relationships based on mutual trust, respect, and confidentiality

- Creating an environment in which personal development is valued and encouraged

- Growing an organization's intellectual assets by sharing knowledge, experience, and expertise in formal and informal partnerships

- Utilizing an organization's wealth of diverse ideas, perspectives, and disciplines

- Creating competitive advantage by expanding the potential and capability of each participating employee

- Integrating the partnering process into business relationships, strengthening it as a cultural asset

- Broadening the internal network of an organization by improving cross-functional relationships

Establishing a coaching and mentoring program provides additional benefits for employees, coaches, and mentors, as well as the organization. Table 8 provides a list of them.

Coaching and mentoring programs help ensure the free flow of information within a business culture. Remember the story of Allen and Malcolm. While Allen took Malcolm under his wing, it was not in a formal mentoring program. Imagine the potential that could have been tapped sooner had the business had in place a systematic coaching and mentoring program. They were lucky that Allen saw the potential in Malcolm and was secure enough in his own position to support him. The change in the production process revolutionized microchip manufacturing.

RELATIONSHIP SKILLS—MANAGING A NEW KIND OF DIVERSITY

The world is shrinking and globalization is a fact of life. Only twenty years ago finding a "Made in China" label would have been fairly rare. Today, a shopper can hardly walk through any store in the world without seeing one. From manufacturers such as 3M, General Motors, and Boeing to retailers such as Wal-Mart, Ikea, and Target to media such as the BBC, CNN, Al-Jazeera, and Fox to local shops and stores, world markets are at our doorstep. While there are yet obstacles to a fully global, operationally integrated free-trade environment, such a global marketplace is not too far out in the future. Business leaders today must figure out how to build enough of the right kinds of diversity into their culture to connect to and profit from a changing world marketplace in the Dual Age of Information and Connections.

In this chapter we refer to building and managing a workforce that is diverse in more ways than age, sex, race, ethnicity, religion, sexual orientation, and nationality. Diversity in the information and connection economy must be broader and deeper than the traditional dimensions of equal employment opportunity, affirmative action, and adverse impact. It is no longer enough to have a workforce that looks like its customer base and the communities in which it operates. The particular kind of diversity that twenty-first-century leaders must be able to manage is the diversity of ideas and opinions and how people express those ideas. Managing this new kind of diversity requires a special set of relationship skills on the part of leaders, because diversity of thought can quickly lead to conflict—conflict that an enterprise leader must be able to manage in a healthy, productive manner. Otherwise, people start throwing ideological spit-wads and verbal rocks at each other.

TABLE 8

Benefits of Establishing a Coaching and Mentoring Program

For employees	<ul><li>Empowers and builds trustworthiness</li><li>Enhances partnering and coaching skills</li><li>Hones skills and abilities</li><li>Builds new relationships</li><li>Gets feedback from various levels within the organization</li><li>Increases personal satisfaction</li></ul>
For coaches/ mentors	<ul><li>Develops skills and abilities to increase professional capabilities</li><li>Gains insights into the organization's culture, history, myths, and heroes</li><li>Increases career planning and personal development opportunities</li><li>Enhances partnering skills</li><li>Builds new relationships</li><li>Increases confidence and open communication</li></ul>
For the organization	<ul><li>Promotes internal knowledge sharing</li><li>Increases teamwork and delivery capabilities</li><li>Aids succession planning</li><li>Improves productivity and satisfaction</li><li>Provides firsthand assessment of individual capabilities</li><li>Builds a future-focused, interdependent organization</li></ul>

Core Human Values Override Cultural Nuances

Human cultures are as diverse as the people who inhabit them. Yet despite cultural nuances, humans have many core values that cut across cultural barriers. From Anchorage to Ankara people understand honesty and keeping one's word. From Bangkok to Brussels people understand and value the importance of trust. From Canberra to Calcutta people know a fair deal and whether or not they are being cheated. From Dakar to Duluth people intuitively know if you are being open and candid or closed and secretive. These core human attributes help lubricate your ability to partner in a global economy. Having a staff fluent in these partnering skills will do more to improve your global network than all the transactions in the world. Once the price gets cheaper someplace else, your customers may move elsewhere if you have not established a durable relationship. The cross-cultural diversity that we're talking about goes beyond hiring people who look like our global customers, and includes people who think differently from us, who process information differently, and who are capable of building the kinds of connections that enable business to occur.

Diversity of Opinions and Ideas

One type of diversity typically overlooked is *diversity of opinions and ideas*. For example, we know of a board of directors for a large corporation based in the south-central part of the United States. The board all looks the same—white men, with one exception, a white woman—and, what is more disconcerting, they all think alike. They view the world through the same set of filters. Their values and beliefs mirror each other's. The most devastating trait they share is their dislike for any conflict. As a result of this discomfort with conflict, they never argue over anything. They honestly believe that their ability to avoid conflict enables them to interact in a productive manner. While their interactions may seem polite on the surface, under the veneer of civility they seethe with tension and mistrust. Because they use the style of accommodation with each other to avoid conflict, they have made some huge blunders in their decision-making process. They overlook ethical issues, support cronyism, and make decisions based on a narrow focus of interest . . . their own. The result of the culture they have established on their board is that their organization has overlooked many illegal activities committed by management, and the business has been indicted for criminal activities, including tax avoidance, perjury, and fraud.

Having people who think differently and are free to express their views is an important component of diversity. Without that element challenging and pushing us to achieve more, to continue to be honest, open, and fair-minded, we can sink into an abyss of self-serving behavior that destroys trust and closes down the life blood of the new economy: information and knowledge.

Approaches to Processing Information

How people process information is also critical to having a diverse team. Some people need time to process information, while others do so immediately. Decision making is sometimes as much about timing as it is about the decision itself. Having teams that can respect various decision-making styles is important. Forcing people to make decisions when they are not ready or allowing the decision-making process to drag on too long are equally counterproductive. Making sure there is a balance in your decision-making process not only expedites a decision, but also ensures that the process is thoughtful and participative, building commitment to the outcome and loyalty to the team.

People view the world in limitless ways. As with the evolutionary process, having diversity within an organization is a strategy for continued growth and success. The new kind of diversity means that you will never get so locked into one way of thinking, or viewing the world, that when things change you will be left behind. With the incredible speed of information growth, having a diverse workforce will ensure you're not left behind.

Across the Hall, Across the River, Across the Pond

In a global marketplace, people think differently, act differently, react differently, and do things for reasons that differ from one culture to another—regardless of where they're from. The people of one culture tend to think that the people of other cultures think like them, act like them, and react like them, and that the people of those other cultures do things for exactly the same reasons that they would in their own culture. That assumption is not accurate. Twenty-first-century leaders must learn how to overcome the natural tendency to make that assumption, to counterbalance it with a new set of partnering skills.

Neither an organization's leaders nor its employees acquire the relationship skills to manage the new diversity by osmosis, or by accident, or by divine intervention. Remember the distinction we drew in Chapter 1 between a *culture by design* and a *culture by evolution*? The same kind of design-versus-evolution distinction applies to building the relationship skills needed to transform a company into a Powerhouse Partner. As a leader of an enterprise competing in the twenty-first century, would you prefer that your workforce build relationship skills by design or stumble along with relationship skills by evolution? Which set of skills would you wager has the greater likelihood of enabling your people to achieve your organization's vision, to accomplish its mission, and to carry out its strategic directions? Leaders who want to succeed in managing and leveraging the new kind of diversity must proactively learn, apply, and refine a robust set of partnering skills, and they must ensure that their employees build the partnering skills needed to execute against the strategic framework.

But people in different parts of an enterprise are likely to need different kinds of relationship skills. Partnering with a colleague whose cube is across the hall requires basic partnering skills—interpersonal and perhaps cross-functional skills. Partnering with a colleague, a customer, a supplier, or a strategic business partner whose office is across the river or across the country demands a broader set of partnering skills—interpersonal, cross-functional, and cross-organizational. Partnering with a colleague, customer, supplier, or strategic business partner whose office is across the pond or halfway around the world calls for the highest mix of partnering skills—interpersonal, cross-functional, cross-organizational, and cross-cultural. The farther away a partner is, the greater the need for well-developed relationship skills. Time and distance are relentless adversaries, and you will not overcome them by accident.

KEEPING AND GROWING SMART PARTNERS

Smart partners drive creativity by increasing the frequency, frankness, and fruitfulness of interpersonal connections, dialogue, and collaboration. When employees are treated as trusted partners in an enterprise, they are freed up to pool their collective creative energies for the benefit of the business as a whole. In this chapter we have proposed three concrete action steps organization leaders can take to keep and grow smart partners: build loyalty and a sense of duty; coach people to grow informal communication networks (pathways); and strengthen relationship skills.

Building loyalty is no longer just an option, and top managers must understand that they contribute greatly to their organization's culture. Informal networks serve as the hidden pathways over which information, ideas, and resources can be exchanged in an elusive, fast-moving marketplace. Leaders need relationship skills to manage a new kind of diversity, one of opinions and ideas and approaches to processing information. Employees need relationship skills to enable people not only to tolerate such diversity of perspectives, but also to cherish it as the fuel of creativity. In Chapter 8 we begin our discussion on building the partnering skills of employees, based on a thorough understanding of the Six Partnering Attributes.

8

Reinforcing the Foundation for Openness

We are alone, it seems, because we can know more than we can tell. If we could tell everything, we could become unalone.

—JOHN S. DUNNE, *TIME AND MYTH*

When people congregate in a room and work together, they have a heightened sense of otherness. This dynamic can cause people to react in countless ways, but fundamentally there are three strategies the people in the room can employ: they can work apart; they can work together; or they can engage is a combination of the two. This dance among the three strategies creates tension, generates an energized atmosphere, and ultimately develops into the culture of us. How we dance this dance is important. There is no culture of one. Rather culture is the outcome of the interactions of people and their collective values, beliefs, and behaviors, and how they ultimately morph into something new. These interactions are based on communication and the perception of trust in that communication. Words and actions must be honestly linked.

CULTURE AND COMMUNICATION

When researching an event, historians will often talk about how that incident fit within a greater context. In other words, what were the social, economic, political, technological, and educational conditions and the cultural norms during the period in which the event

Partnering Culture

occurred? For example, during the American Revolution, what inspired some colonials to rise up against the "tyranny" of George III while others continued to maintain loyal to the crown, and still others contented themselves with sitting on the sidelines, minding their own business and waiting to see which way this Declaration of Independence thingy was going to end up? Rooted in the cultural web of Mother England, the loyalists viewed the upstarts as traitors, whereas the revolutionaries—having put down brand-new cultural roots in the new world—considered themselves patriots. What role did the example, the elocution, and the writings of John Adams, Thomas Jefferson, Benjamin Franklin, Thomas Paine, and other champions of liberty play in persuading common folk to take up arms against the crown, in instilling a new culture of democracy, and in chartering a new nation? What role do their words and deeds continue to play today?

In short, those visionary leaders made the business case for a revolution. Understanding what they did and said and how they influenced thought and opinion is instructional in appreciating the power of culture to shape human behavior. Had King George had his own cable news network and a media-savvy communications (spin) director, Americans today might be calling the hoods of their cars bonnets, drinking warm beer by the yard, and heeding (or ignoring) "mind the gap" instead of "watch your step." The obstinate, going-mad-slowly monarch could only see the culture in which he lived; he had no idea that a new culture had been born across the pond and was racing like wildfire across the colonies. Oh, and did we mention that the leaders of the American Revolution walked the talk? Consider the enormous impact of twenty-one-year-old Nathan Hale's final words, "I only regret that I have but one life to lose for my country." Talk about leading by example!

How do the examples of America's founding leaders compare with the examples set by the senior executives of Enron, WorldCom, Tyco, and similar organizations? America's ongoing experiment with democracy has been prospering for more than two hundred years. How long did Enron last? WorldCom ran away from its name and became MCI. As of this writing, Tyco continues to struggle to rebound from million-dollar birthday parties and other excesses.

Leaders create the environment that enables people to achieve or fail. Thus, a leader's ability to create a foundation for openness to other people's ideas, thoughts, perceptions, information, beliefs, and values is a critical component in creating a diverse culture of ideas. Silencing people by intimidation and fear only limits a leader's ability to be successful in the Dual Age of Information and Connections. Openness within the culture is established through communication, including self-disclosure and feedback and the building of trust.

Self-Disclosure and Feedback and the Ability to Trust

The smart partnering attributes Self-Disclosure and Feedback and Ability to Trust are intertwined. Words and action bond together and result in trust. When we say we are going to do something and then do it, we build trust. If we don't do it, we damage trust. Others will view us as either trustworthy or untrustworthy based on whether what we do is consistent with what we say.

Bob is constantly telling his boss Sue that he intends to call on a difficult customer. The days turn into weeks, and Bob still has not called on the customer. Sue follows up on a weekly basis. After about a month, Sue tells Bob not to bother and asks Mark to follow up with the difficult customer. Sue no longer trusts that Bob will follow up. Bob is disappointed that Sue took the responsibility away from him and claims he had every intention of calling on the customer. But Sue simply didn't believe Bob anymore. "He just doesn't want to call on the customer, and even though it's his job, I can't make him do it. It's easier to give the job to someone else."

This sort of situation points out two different types of trust: task and relationship. Sue does not trust Bob to accomplish the task she expects him to do, but she has also lost confidence in her relationship with him, hence the avoidance strategy. These two areas of trust are not always linked. For example, Sue may trust Bob to support her in a meeting (a relationship issue), but not trust him to call on the difficult customer (a task issue)—or the other way around. In either situation trust is diminished. When both a lack of trust in the relationship and a lack of trust that the task will get done are present, the overall level of trust is greatly diminished.

Two strategies for building a foundation for openness within the business are cultivating self-disclosure and feedback and making a conscientious effort at building, sustaining, and measuring trust; the two are interrelated. Let's start with self-disclosure and feedback.

SELF-DISCLOSURE AND FEEDBACK— THE KEYSTONE OF COMMUNICATION

In the example above, Sue missed an opportunity to practice her self-disclosure and feedback skills. She had a chance to tell Bob how his reluctance to call on the difficult customer made her feel. Maybe she was feeling dismissed or disrespected by Bob. Since she is Bob's boss, perhaps she felt he was being insubordinate. Regardless of what Sue was feeling, she missed the opportunity to have the discussion with Bob and instead wrote him off as untrustworthy. Is Bob untrustworthy, or is there more to the story?

This example illustrates why mastering the art of self-disclosure and feedback is critical to business success. Taking the time to communicate with Bob and creating a safe, open, two-way dialogue would have generated the flow of information between two conduits of intelligence. Bob may have been reluctant to call on the customer for a variety of reasons unknown to Sue. Perhaps the customer was not interested in the product or service, or had acted in ways that offended or hurt Bob and the company. Perhaps there were relationship issues between Bob and the customer. Bob may have been uncomfortable in sharing these issues with Sue, or may have not even understood them himself. No matter the reason, what Sue ended up with was silence. She cut off communication with Bob, declared him untrustworthy, and so began the downward cycle of broken trust.

How often does this kind of situation happen in your business? With compressed timelines, looming deadlines, and more work than there are people or time to do it, who has the time to explore the dynamics of a seemingly minor incident? When creating a foundation for openness, it is precisely these types of situations that require our attention. Why? Taking the difficult customer away from Bob and giving the call to Mark was like the example of the pebble tossed in the pond we used in Chapter 1. Sue sent a message—never mind that it was vague and unclear. What others saw was that Bob was taken off and Mark put on, with no reason given. Sue simply didn't want to invest any more energy in understanding why Bob was refusing to call on the customer. Her frustration with Bob won out, and they both lost. Bob never had the opportunity to explore with his boss his reluctance to call on the customer, and Sue lost the opportunity to learn more about the issue. Altogether, this incident was an important opportunity to share intelligence and a missed opportunity to problem-solve, build win-win solutions, and, most important, restore trust.

The JoHari Window—Building a Culture of Trust

The JoHari Window (see Figure 8), the model developed by and named for Joseph Luft and Harry Ingham, can help demonstrate how self-disclosure and feedback and the ability to trust are interrelated. It can also help us to understand the complexity of self-awareness and communication.

Stephen Dent's book *Partnering Intelligence: Creating Value for Your Business by Building Strong Alliances* details how the model can

FIGURE 8
The JoHari Window

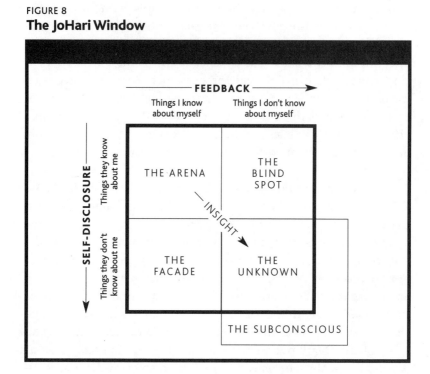

be used for building trust at both the individual and team level. The principles are relevant at the organization and cultural level as well. When people get to know each other and have similar amounts of information about each other, they are more likely to have things in common. Although we may find the notion disturbing, human beings are hard-wired to be more comfortable around people who are like them. These similarities become the foundation for the development of trust.

In a business culture, information flows freely when people feel comfortable and trust those with whom they are communicating—otherwise they tend to hold information close to the vest and not share as much. If an organization is filled with people who are reluctant to trust and do not share information freely, opportunities can be lost. But more important, opportunities can simply go unrecognized due to lack of communication.

The JoHari Window demonstrates how improving our ability to self-disclose and provide feedback can help us explore the unknown, create opportunity, and improve the bottom line. The four "panes" of the JoHari Window—the Arena, the Blind Spot, the Facade, and the Unknown—each represent an element of ourselves and how others might see us.

The Arena

The Arena represents the aspect of yourself that both you and your partner know about each other. For example, you may know each other's job title, but do you really understand the roles and responsibilities that each of you have in the organization? The most productive relationships have large Arenas because a great deal of information sharing is occurring and both partners know a lot about each other and demonstrate a balance between self-disclosure and feedback. Powerhouse Partners understand that the more information is shared, the greater the opportunity to generate business.

The Blind Spot

We never like to admit it, but we all have a Blind Spot, where others can see something in us that we cannot. When you provide me with feedback, you are reducing my Blind Spot and widening our Arena. While I may not like your pointing out behaviors that I may not be aware of or that may not be flattering, it is important that I see myself the way others do and decide if I want to change the behavior.

The Facade

The Facade serves to hide our secret side, one that only we know about. It may be something personal, or something business related, or both. For example, I may not be a trusting person naturally. My style may be such that you have to earn my trust. If I fail to disclose that you must earn my trust, you may never understand why I am always checking up on you. The usual outcome is that you become resentful of my checking up on you all the time and begin not to trust me. However, if when we first meet I explain that you will have to earn my trust and that until that time I will check up on you, while you may not like it, at least you will understand my behavior. By sharing this information with you I have lowered my Facade and increased our Arena.

The Unknown

The Unknown is the land of opportunity. Despite the old adage, what we don't know can hurt us. Getting to the Unknown involves the confluence of information sharing, creativity, and insight. It's what moves product development to the next level. It's the new, new thing. It's what your competitors wish they had thought of. But whatever it is, it almost always happens because of a culture that has nurtured people's trust and allowed them to communicate freely and without self-censorship. It's the motherlode of ideas.

The Delight in Discovering the Mysteries of the Unknown

A large national bank, one of our clients, formed a strategic alliance with a human resources company. The bank's goal for the alliance was to transition the daily management of certain HR transactions to the other company. With nearly 140,000 associates, managing the various transactions in the bank required a large outlay of internal resources. The bank's vision was to refocus on its core business competency—helping its customers with financial solutions to achieve their objectives.

Using the smart partnering model and making it a priority to build trust, the two partners began to build a closer relationship. Over time, the bank transferred many transactional operations to the HR company. As the relationship developed and trust was established, they began to share more strategic information about each other's business goals and objectives. During this period, an "aha!" flashed in front of them. Since the human resources company was working closely with other national and international businesses, why not develop a package solution that would enable it to wrap payroll services with banking services, using, of course, its partner, the bank? A total customer solution that benefited both the HR firm's ability to add value, increase market opportunity, and expand its own services while the bank increased its number of corporate payroll accounts. In addition, this offering provided an entrée into these businesses, giving the bank the opportunity to market financial solutions to the HR company's clients.

To some this business relationship may seem like an obvious strategy, but the reality is that the world is full of potential that never is brought to fruition simply because the people involved have never had the conversation—or were afraid to have the conversation—resulting in the big "aha!" It's the combination of creating a culture where self-disclosure and feedback are valued and building trust to enable human creativity and innovation to take root.

Sadly, most innovation is not lost between external partners but is rather stamped out within an organization. One of the hardest jobs a CEO and the leadership team have is to look objectively at their own corporate culture. Some leaders, especially in large enterprises, may develop a superiority complex that shields them from reality and eventually prevents them from seeing the marketplace as it truly is. These businesses are the most vulnerable to self-deception and denial, creating closed cultures that become moribund. These executives have layers of people to protect them from reality, making it close to impossible for them to receive candid and direct feedback. Compounded by the myths that surround them, self-disclosure becomes impossible, as people fear that anything they say might have a negative impact on the business.

The result, using the language of the JoHari model, is a large Blind Spot and a big Facade. The Wizard of Oz can resort to flashing lights, billowing smoke, and a deafening sound system, but these tricks can't mask the vulnerability of a scared old man manipulating levers behind a curtain. How many Great Ozes are posing as masters of our corporations today, and how long will pyrotechnics and empty rhetoric sustain their enterprises?

Recently, the authors interviewed a client to help its leadership team find ways to increase innovation and generate new ideas within the business. The CEO had become frustrated that employees were not coming up with new, better ideas and complained that the workforce seemed to be wallowing in stagnation. When we suggested that the reason for the lack of inspiration might be that he and his staff were not receptive to new ideas and suggestions, we were immediately dismissed. "That's preposterous," we were told. "Of course we're open to new ideas!" he exclaimed as we were walked to the door. We found that experience deliciously ironic. Is it any wonder they haven't seen any new ideas come across their desks? Not only were they not open to new ideas; they didn't even want to hear that they might not be open to new ideas. Small-mindedness is also a self-reinforcing system.

The culture—established and propagated by its leaders—craved what it could not have, and still the leaders were unwilling to think differently about the reasons for the dearth of creativity and innovation. The company's Blind Spot was huge and its Unknown a frightening place. It was easier for them to bounce the consultants and go back to whining.

To assess your own capabilities in self-disclosure and feedback vis-à-vis the JoHari Window, complete Exercise 1 including the score sheet on page 143.

EXERCISE 1
Self-Disclosure and Feedback Assessment

Assessment

Directions:
1. Pick a context for the assessment; for example, a work team, social club, religious group, or family setting.
2. Read each of the nine statements carefully. Think about how often you engage in the behavior described within the context you have selected. Be sure to use the same context for each of the nine statements.
3. Rate each statement based on a scale of 5–2–1 (5 = regularly, 2 = sometimes, 1 = infrequently). Use only the numbers listed (there is no 3 or 4 rating).
4. Enter the rating for each item next to statement in the "Rating" column and total the score on the bottom line.

| 5 = Regularly | 2 = Sometimes | 1 = Infrequently |

Statement	Rating
1. I share my roles and responsibilities with my partner(s).	
2. People give me candid feedback.	
3. I openly share my personal aspirations with people.	
4. I try not to hide unflattering details about my life.	
5. I believe people feel comfortable giving me constructive or critical feedback.	
6. I spend time after weekends and holidays talking about what I did.	
7. I ask people for feedback on my behavior.	
8. I know the recreational passions of my partner(s).	
9. I openly share my mistakes, hoping others will learn from them.	
Total Score	

EXERCISE 1 CONTINUED

Score Sheet

Total Score
34–45 = Large Arena
21–33 = Medium Arena
9–20 = Small Arena

Use the worksheet below to calculate individual scores for your Arena, Blind Spot, and Facade. Enter your ratings for the specific statements indicated.

Statement 1	_____
Statement 6	_____
Statement 8	_____
Arena Subtotal	_____
Statement 2	_____
Statement 5	_____
Statement 7	_____
Blind Spot Subtotal	_____
Statement 3	_____
Statement 4	_____
Statement 9	_____
Facade Subtotal	_____

After completing the score sheet above, transfer the three subtotals—Arena, Blind Spot, and Facade—to the continuation of the exercise on page 144. Then follow the directions to create a personal Self-Disclosure and Feedback Profile. Instructions for interpreting the profile begin here.

INTERPRETING YOUR SELF-DISCLOSURE AND FEEDBACK PROFILE

Now that you have created your Self-Disclosure and Feedback Profile, what does it mean? The assessment measures three components of the attribute Self-Disclosure and Feedback: the Arena, the Blind Spot, and the Facade.

EXERCISE 1 CONTINUED

Self-Disclosure and Feedback Profile

Directions:

1. Enter the three subtotals (Arena, Blind Spot, and Facade) from page 143 in the spaces indicated just above the chart below. The highest possible score for each subtotal is 15.

2. Start with your Arena subtotal. Count diagonally from the upper left-hand corner of the grid at 0 to the lower right and mark your Arena subtotal on the diagonal line.

3. Mark your Blind Spot subtotal on the horizontal line across the top of the grid, counting left to right from 0 in the upper left-hand corner.

4. Mark your Facade subtotal on the vertical line on the left side of the grid, counting top to bottom from 0 in the upper left-hand corner.

5. Create your profile by connecting the three marks. Starting with the Blind Spot mark on the line at the top of the grid, draw a line to the Arena mark on the diagonal line, then over to the Facade mark on the line to the left.

Arena Subtotal _____   Blind Spot Subtotal _____   Facade Subtotal _____

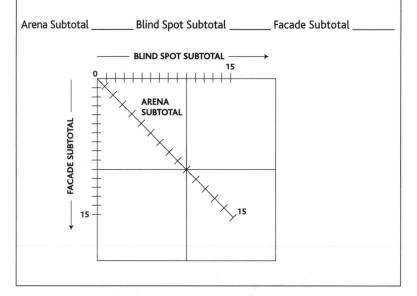

- *The Arena score is your self-perception of what you believe your Arena to be.* Your perception of your Arena may be greater or smaller than either your Blind Spot or your Facade. If such a discrepancy exists, you may want to think about why your self-perception is different from how you actually responded to the statements.

- *The Blind Spot score indicates what is known to others but unknown to you.* The more you seek feedback on your behavior, the larger your Arena and the smaller your Blind Spot. A high Blind Spot score indicates that you seek feedback on a regular basis. A low Blind Spot score suggests that as a rule you avoid feedback.

- *The Facade score indicates what is known to you but hidden from others.* The more you self-disclose information about yourself, the larger your Arena and the smaller your Facade. A high Facade score indicates that you are open to self-disclosing information about yourself. A low Facade score suggests that you generally keep personal information to yourself.

- If your Arena score is lower than the scores of your Blind Spot, Facade, or both, you may have a poor perception of how you come across to others.

- If your Arena score is higher than the scores of your Blind Sport, Facade, or both, you may have an inaccurate perception of how open you truly are to self-disclosure and feedback. You're doing better than you thought!

Create a pane on your profile using just your Blind Spot and Facade scores. Does your Arena score fall inside or outside the pane? Thinking about the Self-Disclosure and Feedback Assessment,

- Does the profile fit with the image you have of yourself?

- Do you think your work colleagues' profiles reflect your image of them?

- How might you improve your comfort with self-disclosure?

- How might you solicit more feedback?

- What do you think the Self-Disclosure and Feedback Profile would look like for your business?

- How does that profile help or hinder you in becoming a Powerhouse Partner?

CREATING AN INFORMATION-SHARING CULTURE

We've been hearing a lot in the news lately about the need for our government's intelligence agencies to share information. A recent congressional report cited the lack of information sharing as a major factor behind the failure of U.S. intelligence agencies to prevent the terrorist attacks of September 11, 2001. To prevent future terrorist attacks, federal, state, and local law enforcement agencies are forming historic collaborations. At the core of these new partnerships is a free exchange of knowledge and ideas about suspected terrorist activities. Many of these agencies will be talking with each other for the first time. Previously, such sharing wasn't part of their organizations' cultures.

Stuck in Smokestack Mode

To be successful, a business, too, must create a culture that promotes the exchange of knowledge and ideas among individuals and departments. Achieving that free flow of information requires letting go of the nineteenth-century industrial business model (where wealth is built on tangible commodities) and embracing a twenty-first-century model (where wealth is built on gathering information about new ways of satisfying customer needs). Unfortunately, too many businesses today still look—internally, at least—like the old "smokestack" industries. Their smokestacks have been transformed into the isolated "silos" that comprise the individual departments within their organization such as Marketing, Engineering, or Human Resources. These departments act independently, without sharing information or ideas, whether strategic, tactical, or technological. As a result, the entire organization suffers.

So how do you create a healthy information-sharing culture within your organization, one that will give your company a competitive edge? You begin by developing a better understanding of why information sharing is so important to businesses today, what causes internal information sharing to shut down, and how a systems approach is crucial to getting the information flowing again.

Information Is Exponential

One of the powerful truths about information is that it is exponential. In other words, if you have information and I have information, together our separate pieces of information can equal more than their sum. Think of it in terms of a jigsaw puzzle. One piece of the puzzle doesn't give you much of a clue as to what the puzzle is about. But when you put two pieces together, you begin to see the pattern emerge. That pattern then leads you to the next piece that must be added, and the next. The more pieces of the puzzle you put together, the more quickly you're able to envision the whole picture and know with even greater precision how each piece fits into the overall design. Business information works the same way. One piece is only a starting point. With each new element of information, you're able to see more clearly the emerging patterns and move more quickly and precisely to make wise—and profitable—business decisions.

The free flow of information within a business can give a company a powerful competitive edge. But employees will share knowledge and ideas only if leaders have created an internal culture that allows them, in fact encourages them, to do so.

When the System Becomes Poisoned

One of the biggest obstacles for leaders to overcome is seeing the business as a series of isolated events. A business is more like a living organism. The health of that organism depends on how employees interact with each other. Without good interaction, employees will not share information—and the company will suffer.

Say, for example, that a conflict occurs between two managers. The company's leaders expect the managers to resolve the conflict in a businesslike manner and to focus on the job. But this kind of "brush-the-problem-under-the-carpet" approach doesn't usually end the conflict. As a result, the tension between the two managers trickles down through the organization and poisons the company's environment, inhibiting the sharing of important information not only between the two individuals, but also between their respective teams. Such a seemingly small episode can seriously harm an organization, especially if the conflict is allowed to be resolved by way of a win-lose outcome.

Let's take a closer look at how the organization is harmed. When people are in conflict, they are rarely comfortable revealing their feelings about the underlying issues that led to the conflict. Nor do they feel comfortable giving feedback, especially if the other person is in a position of power. Trust within the organization quickly diminishes, making any future interaction between the parties even more difficult. So a small conflict can grow like crabgrass, infiltrating an organization and creating an environment that shuts down communication and the sharing of ideas.

Remember: In the Dual Age of Information and Connections, information is the raw material that gives businesses their competitive edge. Each day without open internal communication is a day of lost business opportunity. Why? Because today's news is tomorrow's history. Knowledge and information have a shelf life, and if they're not used while fresh, they quickly go stale. If you fail to communicate and use information while it's relevant, you will lose the advantage that the information offered you. That's why it's imperative that an organization's environment be receptive to building the kinds of internal partnerships that allow information to flow freely and without inhibition. Self-Disclosure and Feedback and Ability to Trust are the foundational attributes for keeping information flowing, though as you will see in Chapters 9 and 10 there are other crucial attributes involved.

A Systems Approach

Creating internal partnerships has never been more critical. In the past, when teams of employees worked in conjunction with each other on assembly lines, they really didn't need to share much knowledge. Just working on a task together was challenging enough. In today's information and connection enterprises, sharing information is more intimate, requiring people to have more developed interpersonal skills. Those skills don't come naturally to everyone, as most managers know—nor is there only one skill that people need to learn for internal partnerships to work.

Ensuring a free flow of information within an organization requires a systems approach. You can't work on only one problem area—improving employee feedback, for example—without also working on others, such as building trust and developing comfort with change. Information will stop flowing unless all areas of the system are addressed. That's where the knowledge of the Six Partnering Attributes can be tremendously helpful. Developing these interconnected attributes—Self-Disclosure and Feedback, Win-Win Orientation, Ability to Trust, Future Orientation, Comfort with Change, and Comfort with Interdependence—can enable an organization to resolve its internal conflicts in a healthy, positive way, moving it toward a partnering culture. The results can be stunning: a free, open flow of information and ideas within your organization—and a new and exciting competitive edge.

ABILITY TO TRUST—
THE CORNERSTONE OF CONNECTION

Some executives give lip service to the importance of trust but fail to see a direct connection between their own behavior and the amount of trust people have in their organization. The impact of corporate executives' inability to build trust goes far beyond their immediate employees. The stock market slide of 2001–2002 was, to a large degree, due to the lack of investor confidence in accounting and financial reporting practices. Investors didn't trust the numbers being produced by CFOs, who they felt were misrepresenting the economic health of their companies.

But not trusting the numbers really means not trusting the people behind the numbers. This mistrust of business leaders translates directly to investor reluctance to invest, which then denies businesses access to the capital they need to grow, which then hurts their employees and the overall economy. It's a vicious cycle in which everyone loses.

Trust Building Is Not a Passive Activity

A direct correlation exists between how employees view their company and how customers and stockholders view it. Once leaders have lost the confidence of employees, that negative energy has a measurable impact on the messages employees—and especially frontline employees—deliver to customers, the community at large, and stock-holders. Executives must take an active role in leading the discussion about trust in their organization. This dialogue is not something to be left to Human Resources or Public Relations. And it has to be more than platitudes on a wall.

Trust is a broad term that encompasses many emotions and has many definitions. Leaders first have to know what their employees mean when they talk about trust. Are they referring to the executives' ability to manage the business, or their ability to be candid about the state of the company? While related, these questions stem from two very different aspects of trust.

Task and Relationship Elements of Trust

Building trust has two components: task and relationship. The task component of trust is about believing that others will do what is expected of them. When we question whether someone can complete a project on time or has the skills to reach a goal, this concern reveals unease about the task component of trust. We have identified five competencies that help to build task-related trust:

- Staying committed to agreements

- Possessing the required skills

- Achieving consistent output

- Making contributions

- Collaborating on projects

The relationship component of trust is about believing that others want a safe and supportive relationship with you. When we don't believe someone will be candid with us or show compassion toward us, this apprehension reveals a weakness in the relationship component. The five elements of trust for the relationship component are

- Staying committed to the partnership

- Showing the ability to be candid

- Being willing to communicate

- Showing compassion

- Demonstrating personal credibility and integrity

Understanding these components of trust will help you create a foundation for discussing what trust means to your organization.

Establishing a First Line of Defense

Defining trust is always the first step. Once you've defined what trust means to your organization, you can go about establishing a first line of defense against mistrust. First, identify specific behaviors that either support or diminish trust in the company. For example, for the task component of trust you might determine that completing projects on time is a trust-building behavior. While this seems obvious, many people do not make the connection that delivering projects late destroys trust among people. In fact, in some businesses, project deadlines are falsely inflated to compensate for late deliverables. This practice is not only costly, but can also hurt your business's reputation.

For the relationship component of trust, you might find that candid communication is vital. For example, you might discover that you build trust every time you don't put spin on bad news. People typically see through spin anyway, which puts a double hit on your credibility.

Making Trust an Important Organizational Measurement

You can measure trust just like you measure product quality or customer service excellence. Remember the old saying: People do what they are measured to do. It's true! If you don't measure trust, you risk sending the message that trust is not important to you. Trust is simple to measure—just ask. An anonymous survey will reveal whether trust is being built or eroded in your organization. Communicate the survey results to your organization and track trust regularly. When you see the amount of trust backsliding, ask why. Also check yourself to make sure you really want to hear the truth. Such an occasion might be a good time to review your self-disclosure and feedback skills.

A trust indicator can let you know in advance if something is weakening trust in your business. The sooner you know, the quicker you can address it. This tracking of trust is a small investment in maintaining morale, keeping information lines open, and maintaining your good reputation in the marketplace. You'll see the benefits in employee productivity, customer satisfaction, and, yes, stockholder confidence. How much is that worth to you?

The Fallout from Enron: It's a Matter of Trust

The collapse of Enron and other companies has been having ripple effects throughout corporations across the country. In companies large and small, employees have begun to harbor serious doubts about the integrity of their leaders and about whether their own financial future is protected. If these doubts are allowed to grow and fester, two things will happen:

- **Communication will shut down.** When employees feel betrayed, they stop talking to their managers. This clamming up can have a negative effect on an organization, because when employees stop giving their feedback, ideas stop flowing as well.

- **Creativity will cease.** When people don't feel trust, they stop taking risks. Without risk taking, creativity doesn't happen. The impact on an organization can be crippling. That's because in an information and connection economy, the ability to use information creatively is the key to organizational success—and to satisfying customers.

A Two-Way Conversation

You can head off such problems—or repair these problems if they already exist—by talking about trust with your employees. Unfortunately, most organizations don't discuss trust issues, or if they do, it's usually about what the *employees* should do to ensure the company's trust. What companies frequently fail to understand is that trust is a two-way conversation. Yes, you must have trust in your employees, but it's also true that your employees must have trust in you.

Examining Your Ability to Trust

People tend to approach trust from one of three perspectives. Some people give trust freely until someone else breaks it, in which case they will no longer trust that person. Others withhold trust from the start until the other person earns it over time by demonstrating "trustworthiness" by her or his actions. Still others take a short-term view of trust; on every interaction they "wait and see" what the other person is going to do. None of these three perspectives on trust is inherently right or wrong; each is simply a different approach to building trust. As mentioned earlier in this chapter, however, if your preferred approach is to withhold trust until it's earned by another person, it's crucial that you communicate your perspective on trust to any prospective partner. Otherwise, your partner may think that you will never trust her or him, and this misperception will surely trigger relationship problems that may be difficult to overcome. How do you know how you approach trust?

Exercise 2 is designed to help you and your team better understand the team's various perspectives on the ability to trust. After you and your team members have completed the first part of the exercise, take time to facilitate a discussion of trust among the team. Who gives trust freely? Who withholds trust? Who prefers to wait and see? Does one style govern the team? Next, we suggest that you lead a discussion of how vital trust is to the team's success both in accomplishing its assigned tasks and in building partnerships among the team members. What's the likely impact on customers if mistrust dominates the team? How might mistrust affect the ability of the team to get projects done at spec, safely, on time, and on budget? Once the members of the team feel that they better understand how trust affects what they do every day, ask team members how the team as a whole is doing in building trust with other teams inside the organization. With which other departments is your team having the most difficulty building and maintaining trust? Step by step, you and your team must widen the circle of trust. To what degree do your vendor and suppliers trust your team? Do your customers trust the products and services you deliver to them? In whichever relationship you and your team determine that the team has work to do to build trust, put

EXERCISE 2
Team Trust Exercise

Directions:

1. Distribute the following statements to your team and schedule a meeting to share your responses. The desired outcome of this exercise is a shared understanding of what trust looks like to each of you.

- My ability to trust is (circle one)   High   Medium   Low

- My beliefs about giving trust are _____

- My beliefs about people are _____

- I trust people when   _____

- What my partner has to know about my ability to trust is _____

_____

2. Have each member take a turn sharing his or her response to the first statement. If you'd like, have someone write members' answers on a flip-chart.

3. After everyone has responded to the first statement, debrief the group by asking, "When it comes to trust, what does this mean for our team?" Have a brief discussion and get team consensus. You may want to write the agreements on the flip-chart for future reference.

4. Repeat this process until you have responded to all five statements. This exercise will prepare you for any situation that involves trust with this team in the future.

---

together an action plan for doing so. "What can I do?" you ask. We thought you'd never ask.

What You Can Do to Build Trust

Here, in brief, are four smart partnering steps that can help you to establish trust within your organization:

- *Acknowledge that trust is important to your company.* You—and other company leaders—must be comfortable talking about the issue. You must be able to say to your employees, "It's just as important for you to trust us as it is for us to trust you."

- *Gather feedback about trust from your employees.* Ask your employees to tell you what a trusting work environment looks like to them. Then ask them for ideas on how to build trust in their workplace.

- *Let your employees know what you're doing with their feedback.* Tell them what specific trust-building actions you have decided to take. You can communicate this information in a variety of ways—through an employee newsletter or e-mail, for example, or a companywide broadcast. The important thing is that you close the communication loop and report back to your employees.

- *Make trust a measurable component of success.* You need to know whether the steps you take are actually building trust within your organization. Measuring trust is not as difficult as you might think. You can do it with periodic questionnaires, for example. The key is to keep the conversation going. Address your employees' trust concerns honestly and openly, and listen to their ideas. Remember: You are in a partnership with your employees. Your goal is for them to have as much trust in you as you have in them.

REINFORCING THE FOUNDATION FOR OPENNESS

When building a partnering culture, leaders must start by reinforcing the foundation for openness. Without openness an organization risks not seeing what's going on in the marketplace, with customers, with suppliers, with competitors. Recognizing how the information and connection economy operates is critical. In the Dual Age of Information and Connections people hold the key to business success as they acquire, swap, and transform information into valuable assets for your enterprise and for your customers. Straightforward two-way communication is the conduit—the ability to rapidly exchange fresh, relevant, and potentially valuable information. Openness acts like the "Refresh" button on a Web page. Would you make a buy/sell decision on an equity based on a week-old stock quote? A day-old stock quote? An hour-old stock quote? Trust allows information to flow in a steady stream. It enables team members to become partners and have a sense of shared responsibility for each other's success. How much more powerful would your workforce be if each individual exhibited this sort of trust?

In this chapter we have seen how leaders can reinforce the foundation for openness by strengthening the behaviors associated with the smart partnering attributes Self-Disclosure and Feedback and Ability to Trust. In Chapter 9 we'll see how leaders must next ensure their organization's move to the future with creativity, and how the smart partnering attributes Future Orientation and Comfort with Change can drive that creativity.

9

Moving to the Future with Creativity

No man ever followed his genius till it misled him.

—HENRY DAVID THOREAU, *WALDEN*

Around the world, leaders in forward-thinking corporations are transforming their organization cultures. They're abandoning—finally!—the nineteenth-century industrial business model and replacing it with a new twenty-first-century model. Hierarchies are being replaced with networks. Business leaders are relinquishing the old "command-and-control" approach to managing employees and focusing on collaborative techniques instead. Also being tossed out of executive suite windows is the old competitive win-lose model. Successful businesses are now embracing win-win solutions. One key to being able to make these kinds of cultural adaptations is linked to a leader's ability not only to think about the future, but also to live in the future. Because words and actions form a bond that builds trust, a leader's words must direct the organization's human energy to be future focused. Then, leaders must follow up with forward-looking behaviors that reinforce and solidify a future orientation.

Embedded in future orientation, and linked closely to forward-looking behavior, is the ability to change. We know of many organizations that view themselves as "change masters." In fact, many so-called transformations are merely about shuttering departments, shifting responsibilities, and shuffling people, and they call that change. What's the saying, rearranging the deck chairs on the *Titanic?*

Partnering Culture

The kind of change to which we're referring consists of fundamental, personal change that has a profound impact on core beliefs and allows new language and behaviors to become everyday habits. Once the people within an enterprise integrate these habits into how they do business day in and day out, the organization culture changes. An organization culture is not changed by rearranging the desk chairs on the top floor. It is changed by leaders transforming their everyday behavior.

WHERE A TRANSFORMATION STARTS

If you want to move your organization successfully into the Dual Age of Information and Connections, you must first transform your culture. This kind of transformation is not easy. To change your culture, you must begin to think consciously about and plan for the type of culture you want for your organization. An organization's business model is based on its underlying culture, a culture that is no more—and no less—than the collective values, ethics, and norms of its people. You must start with a review of the organization's strategic framework as developed from the Holistic Organization Model (see Chapter 3). Leaders have the primary responsibility for creating the kind of culture that enables individual, and thus corporate, transformation. The employees then must transform their view of the organization and their role within it.

Unfortunately, business leaders are often part of the problem. They cling to old styles of management while giving only lip service to cultural transformation. This mixed message causes confusion and mistrust within an organization.

Understanding What's New

How do you know when you have truly embraced the new business model? First, you must clearly understand the basic differences between the old industrial model and the new one, as shown in Table 9.

Controlled Production vs. Open Production

Under the old industrial model, companies try to control the material resources they need for production. When Henry Ford needed glass for automobile windscreens, for example, he bought a glass

TABLE 9
The Industrial Age vs. the Dual Age of Information and Connections

INDUSTRIAL AGE (OLD)		DUAL AGE (NEW)
Controlled Production		Open Production
Scarcity Mentality		Abundance Mentality
Hierarchical Structure		Network Structure
Command and Control		Collaboration
Linear/Sequential		Organic/Neural
Win-Lose		Win-Win
Material		Information

manufacturer. When he needed rubber for tires, he bought rubber plantations. He developed a huge business empire. In the Dual Age of Information and Connections, the successful companies focus on their core competencies. To get the materials they need for production, they partner with other companies rather than seek to own them directly. After all, information is the key material in the twenty-first century, and information is so abundant that no company alone can control it.

Scarcity Mentality vs. Abundance Mentality

A scarcity mentality says, "The pie is only so big; so how can I secure my piece of that pie and keep other people from getting it—or even from getting their own piece?" An abundance mentality takes the opposite tack. It says, "The pie is only so big, so how do we make it bigger?" or better, "How can we bake more pies?" Businesses with an abundance mentality look for ways to combine talents and products to create something new and different. An example is the partnership between General Motors and Verizon Wireless to equip certain GM cars with the OnStar™ in-vehicle communications system. GM and Verizon took two products and combined them in a way that expanded the market for both. They made the pie bigger.

Hierarchical Structure vs. Network Structure

In hierarchical organizations, decision making and communication must trudge up and down the bureaucratic towers. That's a slow, inefficient, and often frustrating way to do business. Businesses structured as a network look more like an octopus, disbursing and collecting information to and from a host of sources in many directions at the same time. As a result, these businesses are able to react to the changing marketplace much more quickly and efficiently.

Command and Control vs. Collaboration

Managers in industrial model organizations tell employees what to do and how to do it. Period. It's a management style based on the military chain of command. My way or the highway. In the Dual Age of Information and Connections, forward-looking managers realize that they must collaborate with employees if they want their business to thrive. These leaders open a dialogue with employees and invite input and ideas.

Linear/Sequential vs. Organic/Neural

Industrial Age companies run their business in incremental segments that follow a linear thought pattern. This linearity can lead to dead ends—in ideas and in business growth. Wasted time. Wasted money. Wasted technology. Wasted talent. Another problem with linear thought patterns is that they prevent people from making the kinds of breakthroughs needed to reach new plateaus. Because they are trained in and work in a sequential culture, breaking this mind-set is difficult. As organizations become increasingly information and knowledge based, however, they begin to act more like living organisms. These businesses grow organically or in random spurts, rather than sequentially. Some parts of the business may die, but other parts continue to grow and thrive. Instead of remaining static, the business evolves and adapts to the changing marketplace.

Win-Lose vs. Win-Win

In the traditional competitive business model, there cannot be two winners. For a business to succeed, it must beat its competition. One winner, one loser. Smart businesses, however, are now adopting the win-win approach to competitors. They recognize that there's enough opportunity out there for everybody. As a result of this abundance mentality, they work not to crush their competitors, but to expand the marketplace to everybody's benefit.

Material vs. Information

Under the old industrial model, business wealth was built on commodities—tangible material assets and products. In the Dual Age of Information and Connections, information is the raw material that organizations use to devise new ways of satisfying customer needs—and to grow their business. This shift in perspective represents an important difference from the industrial economy. Although car manufacturers and energy companies, for instance, still produce material products, how those products are engineered, built, marketed, and sold—and the profits they reap—are all based on new and different ways of using information. This change is really what the Dual Age of Information and Connections is about.

Developing the Skills to Make the Transformation

Once you understand where your business needs to go—into the Dual Age of Information and Connections—you need to develop the relationship skills to help move it there. Knowing whether your business culture has a past or future orientation is critical. The new information and connection culture, after all, is a *partnering culture*— living in the past will not enable you to create a culture capable of moving you into the future. Roberta and Jamie's story below illustrates how a past orientation can undermine needed transformation, and how a future orientation can accelerate necessary adaptations to changes in the marketplace.

ROBERTA AND JAMIE AND MOVING TO THE FUTURE

Last week we were having lunch with our friend Roberta, a well-respected banker. Roberta told us about an issue she was having with Jamie, the bank's customer care center manager. It seems that Jamie wanted to reduce the center's call volume by establishing an Internet banking service that would enable people to review account balances, make payments, and transfer money online. We thought it sounded like a great idea, but Roberta was not at all enthusiastic. Her bank, which had a growth strategy based on personalized service, was a phenomenal success, and Roberta didn't want to lose the personal touch that had made the company so successful. Jamie, on the other hand, felt that the bank had to change to meet customer demand. Something had to give! Finally, this slow-burn conflict flared into a full-blown firefight at their most recent staff meeting.

So who was right? Who was wrong? In some ways, the answer to that question is irrelevant. As with many partnering issues, the process is as important, if not more important, than the outcome. The more critical issue here is how the company is handling change.

When things are going well, as they are at Roberta's bank, embracing change can be especially hard to do. But it's also one of the most crucial skills to have. People tend to get complacent when things are going well and take a "don't-rock-the-boat" approach to business strategy. The problem with that strategy is that while you've been drifting along on smooth waters, you've moved downstream and the environment has probably changed. You may have failed to continue scanning the external environment and adapting to new conditions.

Businesses today are facing a colossal transformation in the environment. Everything from the information explosion to globalization is changing the face of the business world. We'll examine how to manage those changes in terms of past and future orientation and then discuss the importance of being comfortable with change.

PAST/FUTURE ORIENTATION AND CHANGE

Roberta believes that personalized customer service, the hallmark of her bank, is only achieved by talking one-on-one with customers. Jamie, however, feels that personalized service can be achieved using many different strategies. Both arguments have merits. The problem with Roberta's point of view is that it's based entirely on previous experience. We must all ask ourselves, How do we move toward the future without becoming trapped in the past?

An orientation toward the past is based on a cognitive brain function called "knowledge transference." From an early age, we learn from experience. If an experience is positive, a positive mental map of the situation is imprinted in our memory. When we run across a similar situation, we react with similar behavior and expect similar positive results. This process works the other way around as well. We remember negative experiences and try not to repeat them— of course with varying degrees of success. Over time, repeated experiences become ingrained beliefs. Roberta believes that a one-on-one customer experience is the only way that her bank can excel in customer service. Period.

However, times change. People change. And ironclad rules can grow squishy over time. It's not that Roberta's point of view is invalid, but it's less valid than it used to be. As we explained to Roberta, "Some people will always want to call and talk to a banker, but others, like us, would prefer to go online. We don't always have time to call during the day, and we like having access to our accounts around the clock, around the country."

Impact on Innovation

The problem is that even good business decisions that provide good results can eventually lead to stagnation. A past orientation among the ranks of leaders is one reason that organizations have difficulty innovating. Roberta's reluctance to support Jamie's online banking concept has an unintended side effect. Everyone in the organization is observing Roberta's reaction to Jamie's initiative. Imagine for a moment how you might feel if you had a revolutionary idea and your boss reacted the way Roberta has. How motivated would you feel to bring the idea forward? Roberta's reaction is the type of subtle message that stifles innovation and maintains the status quo in organizations. If your organization is lacking innovation, it might not be because of a lack of fresh ideas, but rather how poorly new ideas are received.

The irony is that the idea of having a well-staffed call center was once just as radical as Jamie's plan for online banking. Once upon a time, bank managers believed that you could only provide good customer service in the bank lobby. Banking by phone was once thought to be inferior in terms of service to what bank tellers could provide face-to-face. But Jamie knows that you can create a personalized customer experience and build good customer relationships using a technology that is less expensive than a call center. The issue for Jamie, in addition to facing Roberta's past orientation, is her own inability to convince her boss. Jamie assumes that customer needs and technology speak for themselves—which they may—but she also needs to realize that promoting change isn't only about market research data and targeted business results, it's also about the path you take to get there.

FIGURE 9
Three Phases of Managing Change

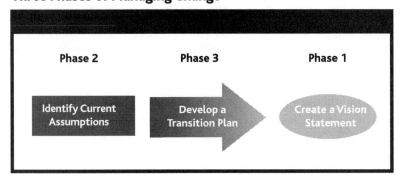

Making the Breakthrough

Not surprisingly, pitting the desire for change against a past orientation can create conflict. People who have a past orientation want to maintain the status quo. They resist change and may even sabotage it. Furthermore, those who want to promote change can often become impatient with those who don't see the future as clearly as they do. The only solution is to partner through the change process. To make the transition from a past to a future orientation, people who resist change must learn to be comfortable doing things differently, to challenge their belief system, and to plan for the future. Figure 9 provides a model for achieving these goals.

Phase 1 is to create a vision statement, a desired future-state on which everyone can agree. Phase 2 is to identify current assumptions, that is, take stock of the beliefs you hold now with an eye toward recognizing those assumptions that may be holding you back. Phase 3 is to develop a transition plan, a set of actions that both parties will take to move the organization toward a future orientation. (Though our example involves only two people, the same rule applies for teams.)

At our request, Roberta and Jamie met with us to work through this model. Together, they created a vision statement of what personalized customer service at the bank should look like. The interesting thing was that when Roberta and Jamie removed their own preconceptions of how customer service would work, both were in complete agreement about what good customer service was. This accord helped them realize that they were clashing over the means but not the ends.

Then, each woman listed her current assumptions about how to achieve quality service. Roberta struggled at first, but eventually acknowledged that she had been defending the call center out of habit more than sound business judgment. Jamie also benefited from this exercise because it forced her to explain how the new technology would work to benefit customers. She realized that for online banking to be as convenient as calling the bank, the Internet banking system would have to have a first-rate design and impeccable security systems in place to instill confidence and trust in customers. Finally, both worked together to develop a plan to meet their mutual vision. What we found most exciting about these sessions was how flexible the formerly resistant Roberta became in the face of Jamie's storm of ideas. "Whoa," Roberta said. "This is great. But let's do this one step at a time." Not too bad for someone who said she wouldn't change.

Viewing Your Environment with a Past or Future Orientation

How do you view your own work environment, your company's culture? Is it oriented toward the past or toward the future? To get a broader view of your corporate culture—and to learn how other people in your company perceive it—share the assessment in Exercise 3 with others in your department or company. The more insights you can get from as many different people as possible, the closer you will get to an accurate view of your culture.

Watch Your Language

Many social scientists and psychologists believe that how people use language helps to shape thoughts, attitudes, and, to some degree, individual personality. Communicating with others in their language can help you to gain insights into how they view the world, their values and cultural assumptions. How you use language—your choice of words and how you structure your thoughts—communicates volumes to them, including your innermost feelings and beliefs. These messages, along with myriad nonverbal clues, are what people grab onto and use to judge the authenticity of your message and thus your trustworthiness. When a leader talks of the future using language that conveys a past orientation, people receive mixed messages.

EXERCISE 3
Past/Future Orientation Assessment

Ask other members of your team to spend a few moments taking this assessment. Then arrange to meet and talk about the results. Are people ready to partner, or do they need to further develop their partnering skills?

Directions:
Following each description below, assign a number value on the graph provided.

1. Win-Lose (Past Orientation) vs. Win-Win (Future Orientation)
A win-lose conflict resolution style creates losers. Losers are neither happy nor satisfied. They want to get even. A win-win conflict resolution and problem-solving style works toward achieving a mutually agreeable plan. Rate your organization on the graph below.

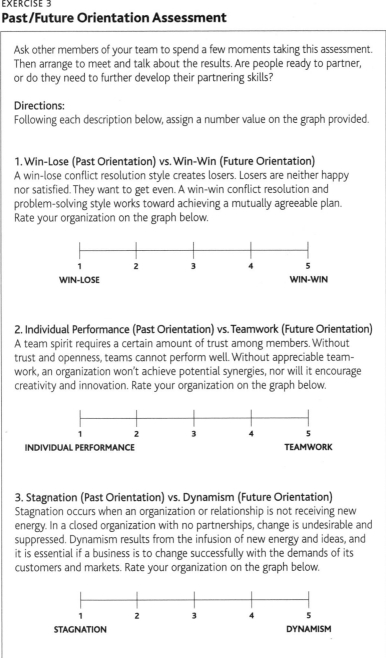

1	2	3	4	5
WIN-LOSE				WIN-WIN

2. Individual Performance (Past Orientation) vs. Teamwork (Future Orientation)
A team spirit requires a certain amount of trust among members. Without trust and openness, teams cannot perform well. Without appreciable teamwork, an organization won't achieve potential synergies, nor will it encourage creativity and innovation. Rate your organization on the graph below.

1	2	3	4	5
INDIVIDUAL PERFORMANCE				TEAMWORK

3. Stagnation (Past Orientation) vs. Dynamism (Future Orientation)
Stagnation occurs when an organization or relationship is not receiving new energy. In a closed organization with no partnerships, change is undesirable and suppressed. Dynamism results from the infusion of new energy and ideas, and it is essential if a business is to change successfully with the demands of its customers and markets. Rate your organization on the graph below.

1	2	3	4	5
STAGNATION				DYNAMISM

EXERCISE 3 CONTINUED
Past/Future Orientation Assessment

4. Alienation (Past Orientation) vs. Collaboration (Future Orientation)
Organizations that isolate themselves cannot form partnerships with others.
There is a lack of trust toward people both inside and outside the organization,
resulting in alienation. Collaboration, on the other hand, involves the give-and-
take of information and a degree of self-disclosure, which results in building
trust between people. Rate your organization on the graph below.

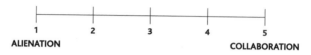

1	2	3	4	5

ALIENATION   **COLLABORATION**

5. Controlling (Past Orientation) vs. Empowering (Future Orientation)
Forming a partnership requires releasing some control over events. If an organization is intent on controlling every aspect of the partnership, the partnership
will fail. Every partnership must be mutually beneficial; therefore, both partners
must make sure they both are benefiting. This means empowering others so they
can work collaboratively toward a mutually satisfying result, rather than trying to
dominate the partnership. Rate your organization on the graph below.

1	2	3	4	5

CONTROLLING   **EMPOWERING**

**6. Deciding from Past Experience (Past Orientation) vs.
Negotiating Future Outcomes (Future Orientation)**
When organizations continue to make decisions based on past experiences,
they limit themselves by not being open to new possibilities. Companies wanting to form partnerships need to be willing to negotiate expectations and then
hold people accountable for doing what they say they'll do. If you continue to
hear statements such as "They'll never do that" or "That's not possible," you
probably work in an organization with a past orientation. Rate your organization on the graph below.

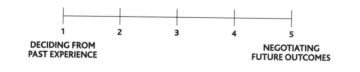

1	2	3	4	5

DECIDING FROM   **NEGOTIATING**
PAST EXPERIENCE   **FUTURE OUTCOMES**

EXERCISE 3 CONTINUED
Past/Future Orientation Assessment

Scoring
Each of the six pairs in this assessment relates to one of the Six Partnering Attributes. Record your rating for each beside the corresponding number below. Then total the numbers at the bottom.

CONTINUUM	PARTNERING ATTRIBUTE
_____ 1. Win-Lose vs. Win-Win	Win-Win Orientation
_____ 2. Individual Performance vs. Teamwork	Ability to Trust
_____ 3. Stagnation vs. Dynamism	Comfort with Change
_____ 4. Alienation vs. Collaboration	Self-Disclosure and Feedback
_____ 5. Controlling vs. Empowering	Comfort with Interdependence
_____ 6. Deciding from Past Experience vs. Negotiating Future Outcomes	Future Orientation
_____ TOTAL	

Interpreting the Results
A rating of less than 3 on any pair indicates that your organization is weak in that attribute. If the total of all six ratings is less than 18, your company may have a culture based on a past orientation. A high overall score on this assessment indicates a future orientation and a strong partnering culture.

For example, what does it mean when a leader praises future expectations while in the same breath berating people for past mistakes? We can address past errors, mistakes, and blunders in ways that encourage people to do better, or at least to match expectations more closely, without shattering egos and turning people into cyborgs.

Table 10 compares some examples of past- and future-oriented language. Which column sounds more like your workplace culture? Think about this list for a moment. If you were to hear a steady barrage of statements like those in the left-hand column, how creative and innovative do you think you and your company would be?

TABLE 10
Past-Oriented vs. Future-Oriented Language

PAST-ORIENTED LANGUAGE	FUTURE-ORIENTED LANGUAGE
"I should've known better than to count on him." "I should never have expected him to pull through." "I knew she wouldn't meet the deadline."	"What do you need to complete the job next time?" "How can I offer clearer instructions next time?" "What kind of time frame do you need?"
"The boss has never been interested in employee input." "I can't believe they gave him such an important job." "Typical. I did all that work for nothing!"	"I know you'll hit the mark this time." "It's an important job . . . how can I assist?" "The boss has promised to implement the recommendations or provide feedback on why he didn't."
"I have never been able to do this." "I've always done it this way; why should I change now?" "You can't teach an old dog new tricks."	"Great, I've been wanting to learn that . . ." "I know you'll do a great job . . . how can I help?" "I can do anything I put my mind to."

Source: Adapted from Stephen M. Dent and Sandra M. Naiman, *The Partnering Intelligence Fieldbook: Tools and Techniques for Building Strong Alliances for Your Business* (Palo Alto, CA: Davies-Black Publishing, 2002).

When using future-oriented language, you must be careful to differentiate the person from the outcome of the past activity. People do fail. They make mistakes and do not live up to expectations. But continuing to focus on errors and not trying to remove obstacles to success is a hallmark of a past orientation. You may find that there are some individuals who simply do not have the skills or natural talents to execute the expected tasks at a high level. Rather than continue to contaminate the culture with negative past-oriented language, it's better to match up individuals with a job that better suits their skills and natural talents.

Language Creates Energy, Resulting in Creativity

In our partner training courses, we conduct an exercise that potently demonstrates how future-oriented language generates energy and vitality—and thus creativity. People have only so much energy to expend at any given time. The more of it your business can capture, direct, and utilize, the more it will benefit.

The exercise goes like this: We put two flip-charts at opposite ends of a room. We title one "Past Orientation" and the other "Future Orientation." We ask people to form a single-file line in front of each flip-chart. The person at the head of the line is given a marker and asked to write a word or phase that comes to mind to represent the title of that flip-chart (either "Past Orientation" or "Future Orientation"). Then, in silence, she or he hands the marker to the next person and moves to the back of the line. This sequence continues until people run out of phrases or words to describe past or future orientation.

We then put the two flip-charts side by side at the front of the room and ask for two volunteers to read the words or phrases out loud to the group, alternating between past and future orientation. Some examples are included in Table 11. Read though the examples in each column. Do you sense different energy levels between the two columns? Try this exercise with your team. Think of the power and impact this simple exercise can have on your business.

Some Closing Thoughts on Future Orientation

Living in the future is one of the most difficult behavior changes leaders must undergo if they are to rewire their business cultures for the Dual Age of Information and Connections. Because knowledge transference is such a powerful hard-wired survival strategy for our species, breaking from past experience and reaching out for something new is difficult. The past grounds us in learning, how we communicate, the assumptions we make about life, and the people around us. But rapidly changing environments require radical new strategies for survival, and we are on the cusp of one of humankind's most revolutionary periods. Never before in our history has so much change occurred in such a short period with such profound impacts on who we are and how we define ourselves. Sticking to business models that were developed by nineteenth-century industrialists will

TABLE 11

Flip-Chart Examples of Past Orientation and Future Orientation

PAST ORIENTATION	FUTURE ORIENTATION
Same old . . . same old	Challenging
Been there, done that	Hopeful
Stagnation	Forward looking
Not again	Untried
Rut	Exciting
Bored	Brand-new
Antique	Promising
Tried and true	Groundbreaking
If it isn't broken, don't fix it	Innovative
We've always done it this way	It's possible
Why change, it's good enough	Imagine the possibilities

relegate your business to history's dustbin, where you can commiserate with fellow travelers from Digital Equipment Corporation, Eastern Airlines, Gulf Oil, NCR, Studebaker, Wang, Westinghouse, and many others.

Our assumptions form the backbone of our orientation. If we continue to make assumptions about people, technology, markets, or anything else based on past experience, beware. Change happens, usually in unexpected ways and at the most inopportune time. As you review your assumptions, be sure you are well grounded in your own values and beliefs, because they will drive your behavior. Check that your values and beliefs are consistent with the values and beliefs you espouse to others. If they are incongruent, others will question your authenticity and trustworthiness.

The world is changing. Keep your mental maps up to date with what is happening in the changing culture both in your own country and around the world. Keep abreast of the latest scientific developments and dare to dream the big dream. Knowledge transference is good up to a point. But to become overly dependent on it without checking out new sources of information is dangerous and could lead down a path of destruction.

Future orientation is learned . . . build a plan for learning it. Most of us are not future oriented. We look to the past for guidance into the future. If you want a future-oriented culture, you will have to educate yourself about your current orientation and make a conscientious effort to change. It will require constant reinforcement and training for your colleagues and staff.

Past orientation can be endemic within organizations. Leadership sets the tone. If you are a past-oriented finger-pointer, don't be surprised if you have an organization full of past-oriented finger-pointers. You get an A for leading by example, but it's the wrong example. To move your business culture from past to future orientation, you must move yourself from a past orientation to a future orientation. This change will be one of life's biggest challenges for you.

Change your language and your attitudes and behaviors will follow. You can start the reorientation of your culture by changing your language. Once you have mastered the change in language, behavioral changes will follow, however slowly. Try not to be impatient. You've had a lifetime to create your past orientation. You won't change it overnight. If you are right-handed, imagine that your life now depended on your becoming left-handed.

FUTURE ORIENTATION AND CHANGE

The dynamics of a past or future orientation and your comfort level with change are interlocked. You may have a past orientation and loathe change. You would really prefer to keep things as they are. Perhaps you embrace change—and strive to initiate it—and therefore believe that you are future oriented. That belief seems reasonable, at least on the surface. However, how and why people embrace change is complex. Change, while causing anxiety for many people in an organization, can be an adrenaline kick for those who enjoy initiating change. While a past orientation is more common than a future orientation, all too often people in organizations create change for the sake of change under the guise of progress. We have identified three different groups of "change agents" based on their different strategies for managing change on a personal level: Initiators, Adjusters, and Rejecters.*

Change Initiators

Initiators of change are people who not only have a high comfort level with change but also see it as an opportunity. They will often do things differently or do different things solely because of their need for change. In most cases, Initiators not only create and/or welcome change, but also do their best to make the change work.

Sample Beliefs and Statements of an Initiator

- Things usually happen for the best. "I think it's great that Mary was appointed to chair the committee."
- Life is exciting when it's unpredictable. "Let's not worry if we don't have our vacation plan all mapped out."
- One should fully experience all life has to offer. "I always want to try new things and go different places."

If you are an Initiator, you find change exciting and tend to encourage it. You have no trouble accomplishing new tasks and working with new people under new and different sets of circumstances. You are always seeking the new and different. However, you must be careful not to impose change for its own sake. Flavor-of-the-month changes can create resistance from partners, undermine the efficiency of the partnership, and damage the partnering relationship itself.

Change Adjusters

Adjusters adopt a "wait-and-see" attitude about change. While they don't enthusiastically embrace change, they are open to it if they see the value and if given enough time. Adjusters want to be sure the change is permanent and necessary. They are more cautious than Initiators and tend to move more slowly when implementing change.

*Descriptions and samples adapted from Dent and Naiman, *The Partnering Intelligence Fieldbook* (2002).

Sample Beliefs and Statements of an Adjuster

- It's easier to function when things are predictable. "I'm not sure this change was really necessary."
- It is best to be cautious. "I don't understand why we're doing things this way."
- One should strive for excellence in everything one does. "I prefer doing things the way I've always done them because I know it works."

If you are an Adjuster, you will initially be hesitant to implement change; but as you learn more and become reassured over time, you will eventually support the change. Since change can represent risk, most people are Adjusters and vary only in the length of time that it takes for them to accept and support a specific change. Be careful not to sabotage the success of the change before giving yourself the opportunity to accept and endorse it.

Change Rejecters

Rejecters refuse to acknowledge any need or value in change. They behave as though external changes have not occurred or are mistakes that need to be corrected. Often, Rejecters campaign to get others to agree with their point of view to "get things back to how they were."

Sample Beliefs and Statements of a Rejecter

- Old dogs can't learn new tricks. "I see no point in trying to find new ways to do things."
- It's important to be in control. "I see no reason to try new approaches when the old way works just fine."
- There are fixed rules for a reason. "Let's do it the way we always have."

If you are a Rejecter, you are extremely uncomfortable with change. Not only might you reject the need for a change, but you may also deny that the change has occurred when it actually has. You may tend to behave the way you always have because you are unable to accept the change. You must be careful not to get left behind or diminish the value of your contributions because you refuse to embrace change. Once a significant number of people—a critical mass—supports a change, the change occurs and Rejecters are left in the dust. To help determine your style of change, take the change assessments in Chapter 6 of *The Partnering Intelligence Fieldbook: Tools and Techniques for Building Strong Alliances for Your Business* by Stephen M. Dent and Sandra M. Naiman (2002).

PARTNERING FOR CHANGE

All change has a personal impact, especially when it is happening to you. It's a whole lot easier to tell others what and when and why they must change than it is for you to face the change music yourself. Remember: When you push people, people push back. It's much better to have them pulling with you. The potential for a change event to damage trust and create win-lose outcomes is high. Leaders in partnering cultures should follow four simple steps to ensure that when a change event is completed, people still trust them and everyone feels as though they have won:

1. Get clear on the case for change.

2. Align the change with the strategic framework.

3. Integrate the change into the organization structure.

4. Communicate, communicate, communicate.

1. Get Clear on the Case for Change

Get a clear picture of why you want to make the change. Do not rush into the change because it is the fashionable thing to do, or because you have problems you believe a change can resolve, or because you think you will get some immediate benefit. Most sustainable change takes time to become meaningful and to achieve full benefits. Meanwhile, change affects employees, trust, morale, and productivity. First try to determine how much you can afford to lose.

For one of our clients, a state transportation agency, change is pretty much mandated. Each election brings the chance of a new governor, and thus new leaders in the agency. The period after elections is particularly unsettling as the new administration installs its own commissioners to head up agency staff. Recently, this state saw a switch in governors, majority party rule, and the department's operational philosophy. One of the new administration's election pledges was to increase road construction to relieve suburban congestion. This commitment coincided with a period of financial duress in the state due to a slow economy. The previous administration's transportation policy favored multiple modes of transportation and unconventional projects such as creating bike trails. The new administration campaigned on a promise to improve existing highways and to increase capacity. For close to a year, the department was paralyzed, however, due to leadership's lack of clarity on why they wanted the change. Key leaders within the new administration had broad concepts in mind, but their vision was too undefined and intangible for engineers, project planners, and bureaucrats to understand clearly the nature of the new direction. To compound the problem, the state was planning layoffs within the department, the first in its history.

Change was happening throughout the agency, and the reasons for the change became mired in the confusion of the situation. People in the agency didn't understand why change was happening when they were proud of their record of accomplishment, and layoffs smelled to them like political payback. Government bureaucracy prevented the new administration from managing events fast enough, resulting in anxiety and fear in the agency. Millions of dollars were wasted due to plummeting productivity as employees spent hours and hours standing around the watercooler wondering about their fate, trying to figure out what was really going on. Their bosses simply couldn't stop such counterproductive behaviors because they were doing precisely the same thing. Although road maintenance continued, internal administration slowed down or stopped while everyone was trying to understand the new agency's vision and role, and how each individual fit into the bigger picture.

Leaders should have been clearer about each change event that was occurring. For example, downsizing was an economic reality due to depressed state revenues. The new vision of the agency was to concentrate on building more roads. Although agency employees may not have agreed with the direction, at least they would have been clear about it. Had leaders been clear about the new vision and why the change was necessary, the agency could have been more productive more quickly, putting the new administration's plan to work sooner.

2. Align the Change with the Strategic Framework

Trying to implement change that is inconsistent with the values and strategic direction of an organization can be devastating. In the example of the transportation agency, most of the employees felt that creating a multimodal transportation system was superior to simply building more roads. What the new administration was trying to accomplish went against the values of the people who worked in the agency, who felt that building more roads was not the answer to urban congestion. There were too many examples of that strategy being tried and failing to support the new governor's plan. In addition, the agency had developed a ten-year transportation strategy for the state, complete with vision, mission, and strategic directions. When they were asked to abandon the strategic framework they had spent years trying to make happen, they refused. Not deliberately, or with insubordination, but through subtle, more effective ways of preventing change from happening.

To a person, they were proud of their network of highways, and fiercely defended the high quality of work and the maintenance programs they had in place to ensure that the highways were in excellent shape year-round. They were not anti-highway people by a long shot. They were simply overwhelmed at the overarching change that occurred when the new administration took office. The new administration also failed in its attempt to implement the change in two ways. First, they failed to articulate the case for the new vision and to deliver reassuring messages that people would still be doing fundamentally the same things they had been doing. Second, they failed to understand the values of the people who worked in the transportation agency. These are professional people who are proud of their accomplishments, and who felt that the new administration was belittling their judgment, reputation, and accomplishments.

3. Integrate the Change into the Organization Structure

When planning for a change event, you must integrate the change into the organization structure by enlisting representatives from each department or team, communicate the planned upcoming change, and—using your self-disclosure and feedback skills—describe the impact the change will have on each group. As the impact becomes clear, put together teams to develop win-win outcomes and plans to mitigate any destructive backlash or sabotage that may arise. Remember, having people pulling with you sure beats having people pushing against you.

Using the state transportation agency example, what might the outcome have been if the new administration had gone to each department, shared the new vision of how they wanted the agency to operate, and then asked each department to think of ways to integrate the new operational plan into existing business processes? In many cases, agency bureaucrats were struggling with their own past orientation—they've always done it this way . . . and they know best—and they pushed back against the change. Agency leaders could have been far more effective by including the departments in problem solving.

For this agency, this particular change event was compounded by the potential of layoffs. State revenues had declined during the economic slowdown, and for the first time in its history the agency was faced with downsizing.

4. Communicate, Communicate, Communicate

How you communicate a change event is critical to its success. In a partnering culture, communication is key to building trust and win-win outcomes with people. A leader's role is to understand the reasons the change event is important and communicate that business case to the organization, and then listen. How are people reacting? What obstacles are they identifying? What is the impact the event will have on their business process, as well as on suppliers, customers, and others? During this period, leaders should organize formal and informal communication pathways and connections focused only on the change event. The more two-way dialogue between leadership and employees, the higher the likelihood of a successful change.

We cannot stress enough the importance of communication in a partnering culture. It is the foundation for openness, and when change occurs, people take it personally. Communication is your tool for moving from a personal event to a business event connected with the vision, values, and strategies of the organization. A client's CEO, after having led his 15,000-person organization through a gut-wrenching reorganization, remarked, "What I have learned from this process is that in this kind of process a leader can fail to communicate, or a leader can undercommunicate, or a leader can miscommunicate, but in this kind of process a leader cannot overcommunicate."

Who's Accountable?

When things go wrong, leaders are ultimately accountable. Powerhouse Partners know that there must be someone or some group responsible and accountable for overseeing the change event—and must "own" the change. Change owners must feel passionate about the event and dedicated to ensuring that the event achieves its objectives. Their commitment must be unwavering. As the army drums into the heads of all its young officers, "A commander is responsible for everything the troops do, or fail to do." No exceptions. No buts. No excuses.

Chaos Happens

Change and chaos go hand in hand. The more dramatic the change, the bigger the organization, and the greater the number of people involved, the more chaos you can expect to occur. Powerhouse Partners know that during this time of transition the key to success is letting go of fear. Change brings unknown situations, and fearing the unknown is an innate human trait. So before the event occurs, prepare yourself to do the following things:

- Understand your point of control and figure out personal strategies to operate within the things you can control. Then, let go of issues that are outside your control. Why waste energy and anxiety on things you have no power over? When you as the leader are anxious and become overcontrolling to compensate for the lack of control, you send negative energy throughout your organization.

- Rather than fret over the perception that you may lose power due to the change event, take stock in the power you have and use it to make the change event better for those around you.

- Think about the level of consistency you need, whether it's in product output, relationships, communications, or processes, and then create a plan for preserving what does not have to change. Change causes things to happen in unpredictable ways. If you need a high degree of consistency in life, change will be difficult for you.

- Let go of the status quo. Change is about remaking the status quo, and things will never be the same again. Growth is a good thing, isn't it? Consider your future orientation.

- Measure a change event not only by the success of implementation, but also by preservation of trust within the organization. If you implement a new system but lose the trust of the people, what have you truly gained?

Comfort with change and a future orientation go hand-in-hand in helping your business become a powerhouse of creativity. But that creativity will occur only if you create an open and receptive environment to facilitate the flow of human energy within the organization. This flow can be easily clogged or stopped. Make sure you do all the necessary things to keep positive, trusting energy flowing during your change event and continue to focus on the future. Big dreams do come true.

With the organization positioned to move to the future with creativity, leaders must next ensure that their organization can embrace connectivity for agility. In Chapter 10 we discuss how the smart partnering attributes Win-Win Orientation and Comfort with Interdependence combine to boost agility.

10

Embracing Connectivity for Agility

We glide past each other. But why? Why—? We reach out towards the other. In vain—because we have never dared to give ourselves.

—DAG HAMMARSKJÖLD, *MARKINGS*

In Chapter 8 we discussed the importance of building a foundation of openness through improved personal communication skills—self-disclosure and feedback—and understanding the importance of defining, building, sustaining, and measuring trust within an enterprise as the foundation of a partnering culture. We also demonstrated how these two competencies are inseparably linked, creating a powerful bond between word and action, resulting in trust. In Chapter 9 we added to the blueprint for building a partnering culture by stressing the need to create a future orientation—both with people and business operations—which gives leaders the creativity and adaptability needed to reconnect smoothly in new, unexpected ways when market conditions change. In this chapter we complete the blueprint by explaining why leaders must embrace connectivity to gain agility with a win-win orientation and by embedding a mutual sense of loyalty through interdependence.

AN UNNATURAL ACT

Many business executives operate under the false assumption that partnering skills are innate. These leaders regard themselves as great partners—now, if they could only "fix" everyone else. Partnering, however, is actually an unnatural act for most people. The relationship

Partnering Culture

skills required for being a great partner and building a partnering culture are counterintuitive to much of what we've been taught, how we've been socialized, and how we've been rewarded both in our personal and professional lives. Take a close look at how the media constantly bombard us with messages that deride partnering in favor of going it alone. Think of a favorite movie hero. How much alliance building did he engage in to outsmart the bad guys? Not much, probably.

So it's not surprising that the Western command-and-control business model—so prevalent in global enterprises—for the most part portrays business heroes and heroines as strong, silent, independent, competitive types. Rugged individualists. According to this model, the "good guys" get the best of every deal, outsmart their partners as well as their competitors, and ride roughshod over anybody who gets in their way. Leadership as heroism. Winning isn't just everything, it's the only thing. Or is it? Such winner-take-all competitiveness may be necessary for a movie plot or for victory on a football field, but in the world of business, this scarcity mentality tends to focus on the short term and is destined to lead to failure.

In this book we have continued to stress a leader's role in building trust in an organization. However, during the past two decades the concept of trusting employees to pull their weight in tough times has fallen out of favor. Instead, many executives have focused on short-term strategies such as downsizing, outsourcing, and mergers and acquisitions to grow revenues. These revenue-enhancing tactics can deeply disturb the partnership between leaders and employees, and often create as many problems as they solve. It's a mistake to say these short-term strategies are inherently wrong. They're not. Rather, it's the way in which they have been implemented that undermines employee morale, costing companies billions in lost productivity and poor customer service, and resulting in the downfall of business empires. One need only review the litany of failed, or failing, business alliances—AOL and Time/Warner, AT&T and NCR, Exxon and Reliance Electric, FPL and Colonial Penn, IBM and Rolm, Mobil and Montgomery Ward, Novell and WordPerfect, to name a few.

Often, the underlying message leaders inadvertently send is that the needs of the business and the needs and desires of the employees are completely at odds, often irreconcilable. We do not believe this perspective to be the case. Businesses that have embedded a partnering culture within the organization have the relationship skills they need—both in their leaders and their employees—to weather these kinds of storms without fear. How? In the Dual Age of Information and Connections, businesses by necessity must reach out, form business relationships, profit from them, and move on quickly. Propagate connections. Having a culture that is grounded in trust, able to communicate, and focused on the future will give your enterprise a competitive advantage for doing just that. While competitors are squabbling over internal issues, baffled by confusing communications, and mired in mistrust, your Powerhouse Partner will be poised to take advantage of the ever-changing marketplace, leaving competitors behind wondering, "What happened?" Little would they suspect you have an enabling culture designed for just that strategic approach.

One possible unintended consequence of these often necessary actions is to create a gulf between leadership and employees. Employees sit paralyzed as they wait for the next shoe to drop. They feel as if they're being tagged as a part of the problem rather than being sought out as a potential part of the solution. Leaders often respond not by trying to understand but by fostering a climate of fear to force results. What they get instead is minimum compliance, not nearly enough to sustain any business for the long haul. Are we doomed to this lose-lose scenario? We don't believe it has to be this way. In this chapter we show you how leaders can attain the hard business results they require while keeping a productive and loyal workforce through the use of win-win attitudes and teamwork excellence.

A Quandary for Leaders

Never in modern business history have leaders been faced with such thorny dilemmas. Consumers want more for less, while top executives, shareholders, and "the street" demand ever-greater return on investment. This predicament is compounded by a workforce that expects more personal satisfaction from work and will leave in a heartbeat if their needs aren't being met, taking with them business strategies, product rollout plans, hard-earned customers, and relationships with partners, suppliers, and the community. And then they come back to poach other dissatisfied employees because they know exactly who they are and what it will take to get them to jump ship.

As if this challenge weren't enough, leaders must continue to make the transition into the Dual Age of Information and Connections. Although information and connections occur in abundance and grow exponentially, in a commodity-based economy scarcity rules, inasmuch as tangible resources are finite. This new economy operates on fundamentally different principles. In the Dual Age of Information and Connections, it's what we share that builds value. And the more we trust people, the more we are willing to share with them, and vice versa. Real wealth is generated by morphing two unrelated pieces of information or relationships into something new and of value to others. Remember the bank and the HR company? Remember the automobile manufacturer and the mobile phone company? They stopped fighting over how to slice the pie and made the pie bigger. Make bigger pies. Make sweeter pies. Make more pies. Make more bigger sweeter pies.

Striking a Balance

Many leaders think they can coerce results. They bully and intimidate, but in reality all they get is the minimum in cooperation and compliance. In the process they unwittingly set the stage for future failure by creating a cycle of conflict and mistrust that becomes increasingly harmful to the human energy of the business, resulting in a culture of losing. Compliance may produce short-term results, but in an era in which creativity sets one company apart from another, compliance isn't enough anymore. An enterprise needs all of its employees' physical, psychological, and creative energy to stand above the crowd.

Smart leaders reject the assertion that there is an inherent conflict between achieving business objectives and satisfying employees' needs. Nothing could be further from the truth. There is a fundamental correlation between satisfied employees and satisfied customers. The key to any leader's success is striking a balance between getting results and satisfying employees' needs.

MANAGING INTERNAL CONFLICTS

A key step in achieving a balance between attaining results and satisfying employees' needs is resolving conflicts using a win-win orientation. A popular myth with executives is that they must be tough to be successful. Although some leaders have gained notoriety by being ruthless, ultimately these top-floor bullies fail because they cannot connect to the spirit of the people who do the work and accomplish the results.

Leadership surveys consistently reveal that the most successful bosses achieve results through connectivity, that is, by listening to people, building partnerships, and resolving internal strife, rather than creating it. While it's true that leaders from time to time must make tough, unpopular decisions, the manner in which they make and implement those decisions will impact their effectiveness. Using a win-win orientation, you may be surprised to discover that achieving results and building a loyal workforce does not necessarily involve a conflict. Increasing employee loyalty could be as easy as listening to employees and acting on their best ideas, an approach that can often bring about exactly the business results you want and need.

Inherent Styles of Conflict Resolution

How leaders act to reduce internal strife depends a great deal on their primary style of conflict resolution. Each of us tends to fall back on an inherent conflict resolution strategy—call it a "default" approach to resolving conflicts. We have identified four inherent styles of conflict resolution:

- **Evader:** avoids conflicts as much as possible

- **Fighter:** competes with others to get his or her way

- **Compromiser:** identifies what can be given up to meet halfway

- **Harmonizer:** gives into the demands of others to keep peace

Each of these conflict resolution styles is based on a form of the fight-or-flight response. This primitive instinct has its uses—after all, we're still around, aren't we?—but it also has limitations. Each style logically produces either a win-lose or a lose-lose outcome; such divisive consequences create either winners and losers or just losers. When leaders apply their inherent, or default, style—the one they often revert to under stress—it's no wonder so many revenue-enhancing strategies end up with someone, and possibly everyone, losing.

Evader

Executives with an Evader style try to avoid conflict with employees. To do this they use a simple strategy: they avoid input from others. If there's no input, then there can be no disagreement. But leaders also lose valuable insights and contributions from employees as well as making employees feel like their work is not valuable. One of the authors once consulted on competency-based selection with a European financial services company in which employees were officially forbidden to communicate with executives. Not only were employees not allowed to speak with anyone whose office was on the top floor, but they were also barred from sending memos to executives and banned from even visiting the top floor (an edict enforced by a stone-faced security guard posted by the elevator). That company is no longer in business today. However, an Evader's defenses against input are generally much more subtle than security guards stationed to shoo people away.

Fighter

Fighters also avoid input from others, but they do it in a more aggressive way. Fighters become so convinced they are right that they become combative whenever they are challenged. If you disagree with them, you are either wrong, stupid, or most likely both! Not the most effective strategy for encouraging input from others. We have all run into this kind of "my way or the highway" manager. In a restructuring engagement in a large American utility, one of the authors encountered a senior vice president determined to ram through an organizational design that he had thought up on a two-hour flight from the company's nuclear plant back to headquarters. He pressed, he pushed, he prodded, and he said no to each and every alternative idea and suggestion. He drove his concept so hard that employees literally rebelled, organized, and forced their way into a board meeting carrying protest signs (as opposed to pitchforks and torches), having of course already alerted the local news media to the impending confrontation. When you push people, people push back.

Compromiser

Being a Compromiser might sound like a positive strategy, but often Compromisers give up on critical issues in order to reach agreement. As a result, they stall having to make tough decisions and often have to deal with bigger problems down the line. In observing a high-level team chartered to restructure the human resources function of a large international manufacturing company, one of the authors got to see firsthand the downstream impact of Compromisers at work. The company had a history of adversarial negotiations with its bargaining units, and so many of its senior HR leaders had become accustomed to seeing compromise as the surest way to gain agreement: the bargaining unit gets a little of this, the company gets a little of that. A zero-sum game in spades. In working with line team members to realign their function, these leaders could not break free of a compromise mentality. As a result, just to be done with it all, the structure team compromised and proposed irrational splits in HR functions, tantamount to Solomon's suggestion of bisecting the baby. No one was happy with any of it, and the CEO pitched most of the team's recommendations and decided himself how things were going to be going forward.

Harmonizer

Harmonizers are the extreme version of the Compromisers. They typically dislike all conflict and would rather give in to others, even at their own expense, than endure the pain that conflict causes them. On the opposite end of the scale from Fighters, Harmonizers would rather just say yes. On a project to build a leadership competency model for a global agricultural products company, one of the authors bumped into a finance and accounting senior manager who dreaded butting heads with the line managers served by her department. To keep these line managers at bay, she had gotten in the habit of routinely saying yes to almost every demand made of her by the senior line leaders, so much so that at one point her staff members, unbeknown to her, spoke of the finance and accounting department as having "thirty-eight number one priorities and no number two-through-ten priorities." Worse for her staff, some of her commitments to provide certain finance and accounting services and reports for one group of senior line leaders contradicted other agreements she had made to please another group of senior executives. The situation was not as bad as having to keep two sets of books, but it was close. The last we heard, that finance and accounting manager had been forced to take a buyout and been replaced with someone who had been able to negotiate the clump of thirty-eight number one priorities down to a much more manageable pod of seven.

The Negotiator Style: Setting the Stage for Win-Win Outcomes

The only style that can produce a win-win outcome is the Negotiator style. Its premise is that to end conflict successfully you must attempt to meet everyone's highest-priority needs. To accomplish this task, leaders must first understand all aspects of the business—from both customer and employee perspectives—using their self-disclosure and feedback skills. They then prioritize the business needs along with employee needs and systematically work to satisfy the key issues for both sides.

While this technique might sound impossible, it's not, and it helps to adopt this strategy in the beginning. When faced with a decision about a proposed revenue-enhancing strategy, you might consider some steps that may at first seem counterintuitive. For example, you might naturally want to be secretive, consulting with a small group of close advisors and planning your course of action with little or no employee input. Instead, we suggest that you begin by opening communication with employees. Talk about the financial and business situation openly and candidly. Employees probably already know what's happening, anyway. Ask for feedback. When you share problems with employees and ask them for help, you'd be amazed at what people can do to conserve resources, create a new product or service, or improve an existing process.

Keep the communication loop open. Tell people what you know—or as much as you can legally tell them—and ask for comments, questions, and concerns. When people feel like they are getting the straight story, trust, credibility, and cooperation grow. Finally, be aware of your conflict resolution style. During times of stress, you will naturally slip into your inherent style. Therefore, it is critical to know and understand this style and to monitor your behavior. If your inherent style encourages a win-lose scenario, or a lose-lose outcome, you will damage the trust and loyalty of your best assets, your employees. Which of the following best describes how you usually go about handling conflicts?

EXERCISE 4
Conflict Resolution Style Descriptions

Directions:
Read the five descriptions of conflict resolution styles below. What is your predominate style when you are in an emotional situation?

1. "I don't like conflicts, and I try to avoid them. I would rather not be forced into a situation where I feel uncomfortable or under stress. When I do find myself in that kind of situation, I say very little, and I leave as soon as possible."

2. "To me, conflicts are challenging. They're like contests or competitions— opportunities for me to come up with solutions. I can usually figure out what needs to be done, and I'm usually right."

3. "I try to see conflicts from both sides. What do I need? What does the other person need? What are the issues involved? I gather as much information as I can, and I keep the lines of communication open. I look for a solution that meets everyone's needs."

4. "When faced with a conflict or even a potential conflict, I tend to back down or give in rather than cause problems. I may not get what I want, but that's a price I'm willing to pay for keeping the peace."

5. "I want to resolve the conflict as quickly as possible. I give up something I want or need, and I expect the other person to do the same. Then we can both move forward."

Interpretation

If you chose description 1 as most characteristic of yourself, your conflict resolution style is Evader, a lose-lose strategy. When one partner avoids a conflict, neither partner has an opportunity to resolve it. Both partners lose.

If you chose description 2, your conflict resolution style is Fighter, a win-lose or lose-win strategy. Either you win and your partner loses, or you lose and your partner wins. It's the survival of the fittest. But conflicts are not contests, and this style precludes the possibility of finding a fair solution.

If you chose description 3, your conflict resolution style is Negotiator, a win-win strategy. Both you and your partner have a chance to express needs and resolve the conflict in a mutually acceptable way. While this strategy may sound simple, it's actually the most difficult to use. It requires each of you to articulate, prioritize, and satisfy your own needs while also addressing the other person's needs.

If you chose description 4, your conflict resolution style is Harmonizer, a lose-win strategy. You lose because your needs aren't met. Your partner's needs are met, but the partnership suffers because you eventually become resentful and unsatisfied.

If you chose description 5, your conflict resolution style is Compromiser, a lose-lose strategy. Both you and your partner give up something you need just to make the conflict "go away." Invariably, you end up addressing the same issues later.

Try the quick Win-Win Assessment (Exercise 5) to determine your primary (default) style of conflict resolution. If you would like to take a more detailed win-win assessment, go to Chapter 3 in *The Partnering Intelligence Fieldbook* by Stephen M. Dent and Sandra M. Naiman.

Moving from a Culture of Individuals to a Culture of Negotiators

Our caveman ancestor Urg was smarter than you think. He may not have been able to articulate his decisions, but that doesn't mean he wasn't always calculating the odds. If he were surprised by a sabertooth tiger and happened to have his spear with him, he might hold his ground. But he was also just as likely to get out of there as fast as his feet would carry him. This fight-or-flight response governed Urg's life—the survival instinct was the only intelligence he needed.

EXERCISE 5
Win-Win Assessment

Directions:
1. Begin by thinking of the kinds of conflicts you encounter.
2. On a scale of 1–6, rate each of the statements below based on how you tend to react to those conflicts. Enter your score for each in the shaded box to the right of the statement.
3. Enter the column totals at the bottom.

| 1 = Strongly Disagree | 2 = Disagree | 3 = Somewhat Disagree |
| 4 = Somewhat Agree | 5 = Agree | 6 = Strongly Agree |

	A	B	C	D
1. I don't give up until the other person agrees with me.				
2. I'd rather fix half the problem than make no progress at all.				
3. I try to make everyone around me happy.				
4. When others are having problems, I mind my own business.				
5. I move others to the middle ground.				
6. I can adjust to any situation and feel good.				
7. When I know I'm right about a problem, I work hard to convince others to see it my way.				
8. It is important to me to avoid arguments.				
Total Score				

Scoring:
Compare the total scores of each column. Your highest score indicates your preferred style of conflict resolution. Your second-highest score is your secondary, or backup, style.

Column A = Evader
Column B = Harmonizer
Column C = Compromiser
Column D = Fighter

What is your conflict resolution style? _____

What is your secondary conflict resolution style? _____

But before we get too comfortable with how far we've come, consider that people today are still ruled by this primal instinct. When confronted with conflict, most of us revert to fight or flight. Of course, over time this response has evolved and become more sophisticated. Even the most contentious boardroom battle doesn't get settled with clubs and shields, although we do occasionally read reports of fisticuffs. Instead of fighting with weapons, we fight with words, or we wield power and influence to get our way. Instead of physically retreating, we might become resistant to change, or settle for mediocrity, or staunchly defend the status quo.

The problem with these tactics is that they create a culture of winners and losers instead of a culture of overall achievement. One of the authors recently attended a board meeting at which team members were reverting to the flight-or-fight response in a way that was ultimately hurting the organization. You would have thought it was back in Urg's day, when the law of the land was eat or be eaten. How do we break free from this programming? Under stress our instincts will lead us to do what is most familiar, but our Partnering Intelligence can help us find solutions that benefit everyone. As we'll see, the answer lies in using our win-win orientation.

Win-Win Orientation Team Profile

Greg is the president of a small Midwestern firm that manufactures medical devices. His executive team consists of Kim, the CFO; Chris, the head of marketing and sales; and Mary, who handles research and development. These executives pride themselves on being nice people who have strong values and ethics and are easy to do business with. However, their work together is being hampered by underlying interpersonal conflict.

Recently Greg asked us for help. When we interviewed the team, it became clear they were having problems resolving conflict. They couldn't agree on anything important; they were avoiding each other; and they stalled on crucial decisions behind a smoke screen of "needing more information." On the surface they were polite to each other, but Mary said that sometimes "you could cut the atmosphere in our meetings with a knife." We began by administering an assessment similar to the one in Exercise 5. Each team member took the assessment individually. The Win-Win Orientation Team Profile shown in Figure 10 represents the results and helps explain why this team was having a problem resolving its issues.

Each of the first four styles—the Evader, the Harmonizer, the Compromiser, and the Fighter—stems from the fight-or-flight response. These are the inherent styles of conflict resolution. The Negotiator style, however, is not a natural response. It can only be learned, and it is this style that is so vital to organizational success. The inherent styles result in either a win-lose or lose-lose outcome, but the Negotiator's primary objective is to create a win-win outcome based on prioritized needs.

The team members with high scores in a particular area are more likely to use that style when resolving conflicts. Conversely, a low score means they are less likely to use that style. To analyze the team profile, look at the highest score in the inherent styles. The style with the highest score represents the team member's primary style of conflict resolution. The style with the second highest score represents their secondary or back-up style.

FIGURE 10
Win-Win Orientation Team Profile (Sample)

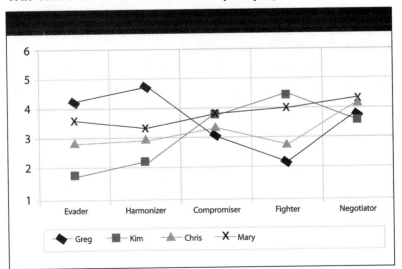

A Quick Analysis

Many people who take the Win-Win Orientation Assessment in *The Partnering Intelligence Fieldbook* (Chapter 3) assume they use a win-win orientation in their dealings with team members. They can all point to times when they used needs-based problem solving similar to the Negotiator style. What they often forget are all the other times when they reverted to their inherent style. The problem is that conflict creates an emotional state. No matter how cool and calm you think you are, when you're in conflict you are influenced by your emotions, and your emotions are responsible for triggering your inherent style.

Looking at Figure 10 and starting with Greg, the president, we can see that his primary style of conflict resolution is Harmonizer. Harmonizers are uncomfortable with conflict. Their managing strategy is to give in to other people's needs to keep the peace. While this seems like a good strategy, over time all that giving in can cause the Harmonizer to be resentful. This bitterness can result in passive-aggressive behavior—such as undermining people because the individual doesn't feel comfortable confronting them in the first place. Greg's secondary style is Evader, which creates a difficult situation for him and his team. When he has a high need but can't harmonize with his direct reports, he avoids the conflict entirely and makes decisions on his own. This tactic alienates his team and intensifies the conflict.

Kim, the CFO, is a classic Fighter. He turns every conflict into a competition, one he plans on winning. Unlike Harmonizers, Fighters are convinced that they're always right, and they will do whatever it takes to win. Kim's secondary style is Compromiser. When he knows he can't win outright, he'll give something up to reach an agreement.

As noted by the relatively straight line, Chris from Sales and Marketing takes a fairly balanced approach to resolving conflict. She moves back and forth between Compromiser and Harmonizer, but she will also become a Fighter if the issue is important enough to her.

Mary, the head of R&D, is also a Fighter, a style that has created an interesting dynamic with Kim. The two of them are always wrestling over the cost-benefit analysis of a particular project. When she and

Kim go at it, the other team members tend to fade into the wood-work until the whole thing blows over. The rest of the team looks to Greg to resolve the issue, but he always seems to give in (usually to Kim if you ask Mary, or to Mary if you ask Kim), or he evades the whole issue entirely.

Getting to a Win-Win Outcome

The problems these conflicts are causing the team are imposing. With two Fighters and two non-Fighters, there is often a "Battle of the Titans," with the non-Fighters sitting on the sidelines, cringing. Add a CEO who is unwilling to engage in conflict at all and it only makes matters worse. What can they do?

First, each team member must strive to understand each other's inherent style. It's a big step, but many teams find that it's actually a relief to talk about the mechanics behind the conflict. Next, the team must acknowledge and understand how emotions are pushing them to revert to these inherent styles. Greg must break through his veil of denial, while Mary and Kim have to stop looking at each other as competitors and start acting as partners. Chris can use her fairly balanced approach to help coach the other team members toward taking the next step, which is moving to the Negotiator style.

The good news is that the assessment indicates that each team member has an intellectual understanding of the Negotiator style. To fully embrace this win-win style, the team will have to consciously decide that they do not want to react to conflict based on emotions. Once they have committed to this collaborative approach, they can take the following steps to achieve a new level of cooperation, commitment, and achievement:

- Acknowledge openly that there is a conflict

- Determine the source of the conflict: Is it based on information, perception, facts, values, or methodology?

- Understand what they consider to be important in resolving the conflict; each team member should write down his or her needs and prioritize them

- Use self-disclosure and feedback skills to share the information among team members and the impact others' needs have on them

- Negotiate the resolution based on getting each team member's most important needs met

Getting to a win-win outcome can be time consuming. But the alternative, creating losers, will ultimately cause you to waste more time and resources than spending the energy up front to resolve the issue and get it behind you. The first time you create a loser on your team, you've set up the dynamic for ongoing conflict.

Leadership Responsibilities

Partnering cultures accomplish conflict resolution and problem solving in a way that enables everyone, regardless of style, to be heard at the table. Everyone has an important contribution—information or connections—that makes their input vital. Using any style other than Negotiator limits the opportunity for everyone to make a contribution. One of the most effective actions you can take to foster the use of the Negotiator style is to set the stage by making it comfortable for people to move to that style:

- Set the tone, in words and actions—let members of the team know that, despite all the inherent styles, you will strive to use the Negotiator style

- Educate people on their inherent style—this insight provides them with awareness and context as they work with others

- Hire smart partners who understand the Negotiator style and can move toward it

- Measure the impact of conflict on the organization and get members to make resolving it an important issue

Measuring Your Win-Win Orientation

We have seen just the beginning of how the Win-Win Orientation Assessment can help your team get on the right track from the start. But the first step in becoming a great Negotiator is awareness. Knowing your team's win-win orientation sets the stage for resolving future conflicts quickly by helping you understand each member's style and providing a context for discussion about conflict styles in general. It is a crucial step toward creating a successful partnering culture. Everyone can agree that collaboration is critical, but how do you measure something as intangible as collaboration? The most direct method we have found is to simply ask people. Survey employees about how well they collaborate with others and how well others collaborate with them. Once you have the baseline measurement, you can then find out how these skills improve over time.

The best secondary indicator of a win-win orientation is how many conflicts escalate to the point where they need to be resolved at the executive level. People who are using a win-win orientation tend to solve their own problems at the lowest organization level possible. If problems keep getting passed up the chain of command for resolution, you know that people aren't collaborating. Establish a measurement for how many issues get escalated to a specific level within your organization. Look for trends. As you track the data, you may discover that one department, group, or person has consistent difficulty collaborating.

MORE THAN TEAMWORK . . . INTERDEPENDENCE

Teamwork by itself doesn't cut it anymore. Sure, teamwork is still important, but in most organizations teams are most often only collections of individuals who come together to contribute individually to an overarching task, complete the task, and disband. They have done their part.

In the Dual Age of Information and Connections, businesses cannot afford to waste one valuable—and expensive—human resource. To be smart and competitive and survive in the interconnected world of the twenty-first century, we have to make sure we succeed and that our partners succeed. We can no longer simply look out for ourselves—we must look out for everyone. The commitment to mutual success must be a part of the culture and embedded in every action we take.

The ability to be comfortable with such a high level of interdependence depends on our ability to master the competencies prefigured by the other five partnering attributes, since each links with the others to form a partnering culture. For example, if you are uncomfortable self-disclosing and offering feedback, you may have difficulty building trust. If you can't build trust, you may have a problem being credible proposing a win-win solution. If you have a past orientation, you may have difficulty accepting change, and so forth. When designing and constructing a partnering culture, you can take specific steps to enable interdependence in the business. Although we have covered most of these steps in previous chapters, we will recap them here as nine reminders to reinforce that if you leave out any component in a system, the system will never be utilized to its full capacity.

Reminder 1: Align Goals and Objectives with Vision and Values

Being clear on the organization's vision and values is the first step. Closely linked with vision and values is clarity on the business's mission and strategic directions. We refer to this series of steps as the strategic framework. It must be shared with everyone from the interview process on and reinforced in as many ways as possible. Help people understand their own personal vision and values and ensure that there is a fit between their intrinsic personal motivation and the mission of the business.

Reminder 2: Communicate with a Passion

While many leaders talk about communication strategies and when to tell what, we believe that leaders must consistently communicate with a passion. The reality is that rumors have probably already worked their way around the office, and people will have gotten an inkling of what's going on anyway. Not sharing information provides grist for the rumor mill; left to their imagination, people will always assume the worst-case scenario. Tell them . . . tell them again . . . and again. You cannot overcommunicate in the Dual Age of Information and Connections. When people do not get information, they make it up. And if what they make up contradicts what you say later, they'll call you a liar. Then when you deny that you're lying, they'll say, "Now I know for sure he's lying." Get ahead of the curve.

Reminder 3: Build Trust

Trust energizes creativity and innovation. Lack of trust drives fear, and fear is a mind-killer. You must build trust—with your customers, suppliers, and most important, your employees—if you want your business to be a credible concern. They are your fountains of information, and you cannot afford to have the spigot turned off.

Reminder 4: Build Diversity in Your Team

Having diversity of race, gender, and so on is great. Having diverse perspectives, ideas, worldviews, and processing styles and having dissention is even better. Worse than having everyone look the same is having everyone think the same. Figure out how to turn differences into strengths and then build on those strengths. Build teams that bring in many viewpoints and manage the creative energy by using communication skills, win-win problem solving, and trust-building exercises to maintain creativity and eliminate fear.

Reminder 5: Encourage Creativity

Creativity generates energy. You have only so much human energy available; use it wisely. Remove fear and give people information and get out of their way. Let them decide how best to use it to serve customers and build value within the business. Let them ply it, shape it, share it, and morph it until you've outdistanced competitors and delighted customers. Your competitors will be scratching their heads wondering how you did it. It's no secret; you've got a dynamic partnering culture that's unbeatable. Linus Pauling, who earned two Nobel prizes, once said in answer to a question about how he came up with so many great ideas, "The secret to coming up with great ideas is to come up with lots and lots of ideas. Then, toss the bad ones out."

Reminder 6: Create Win-Win Outcomes

Never, ever create losers. In the end, the chief loser will be the business. You must craft team behavior and environments so that people walk away feeling like winners, even if they didn't get their way. How you manage dissent and get to the win is critical, and understanding your inherent conflict resolution style and that of your team members is an important tool in getting to that win.

Reminder 7: Let Go of Control

Sometimes, even our best intentions can cause problems. We want the best for our teams. We have a vision of the outcome and what it should look like and do . . . but that doesn't mean we have to control how it is accomplished. Such micromanagement defeats the purpose of teamwork. You must be clear about your vision, articulate your expectations, provide the team with the resources, remove obstacles—which may include yourself—and let them get to work.

Reminder 8: Use the Foundation for Openness

Allow people the opportunity to talk about their feelings, aspirations, and dreams. These elements move a team from the mundane to the extraordinary. Communicate, provide feedback, share information, and dare to dream the big dream. Encourage people to be connected to their work in more ethereal ways than solely contributing to the bottom line—you will be amazed at the outcome. Most everyone would prefer to do well by doing good.

Reminder 9: Weed Out Destructive Forces

Despite a leader's best efforts, negative forces can creep into the organization. You've done your best to hire people with partnering competencies and trained people to master the Six Partnering Attributes, but sometimes people don't fit within a culture, for whatever reason. You must quickly identify and remove them. They can do a lot of damage in a very short time.

With your organization embracing connectivity for agility, you are now positioned to bring all the components of the Powerhouse Partner Model together to create resilience.

Conclusion:
Working Toward Resiliency

The people here come and go so quickly.

—DOROTHY, IN *THE WIZARD OF OZ*

In today's culturally complex, technically intricate global market-place, organization leaders can no longer depend on governance models based on twentieth-century management architectures—hier-archies designed more to disconnect than to connect. People survive and grow by propagating connections to each other and to the world around us. Like our nomadic ancestors who banded together to hunt and gather, we must relearn the art, the skills, and the power of connectivity. Successful leaders must understand and appreciate the profound marketplace implications of the human journey from connections to disconnections to reconnections. Businesses are becoming organic networks, neural webs. Networks grow by propa-gating connections. Connectivity happens when businesses form strategic alliances and partnerships within and between themselves. Alliances produce astonishing results only when information flows freely and people trust each other and are loyal to each other.

Bottom-line business results are rooted in culture. How execu-tives, managers, and employees regard shareholders, how they treat customers, and how they esteem each other all echo cultural rules. How members of an organization go about determining what kind of culture they need to accelerate company growth is itself a cultural gauntlet. Culture springs mainly from how leaders behave: what they say and do, and how they say and do it. Culture is forged and communicated in the messages they send about what is important and what is not important, what is acceptable and not acceptable, and who is valued and who is not valued. Culture plays such a vital role in the success of an organization that leaders can no longer afford to leave it to chance. Yet, as crucial as culture is to bottom-line results, most leaders spend little time reflecting on the constructs or consequences of their culture.

In the twenty-first century, in the Dual Age of Information and Connections, business leaders who want their enterprises to survive, and thrive, must learn the lessons of a designed culture. Culture by design happens when leaders sit down and formulate a culture and then rigorously communicate and live by its tenets. Cultures that have been designed to champion a powerful purpose stand the test of time. Few businesses have consciously taken this purposeful path, though some have had the advantage of having leaders with an unconscious competency in this area. Leaders must think resolutely and thoughtfully about the atmosphere, environment, and customs that they want to permeate their organizational environs. In their gut, they must "get" the connection of their organization's purpose and the culture required to sustain that purpose. Moreover, they must take stock of their own abilities and willingness to model the attitudes and behaviors they are seeking and realistically assess if they are truly behaving as they want others to behave. Just think of the CEO who says he wants to establish a culture of openness and trust but who then summons the vice president of marketing and sales to his office and berates her for falling sales.

WHAT DOES A POWERHOUSE PARTNER LOOK LIKE?

In today's economic environment connectivity is critical for any business aspiring to be a true Powerhouse Partner. The ability to partner successfully has an impact on every aspect of an organization's culture and operations—from its strategic framework, through its business processes, to its human resources strategy, resulting in a workplace where people want to stay and to which they will contribute their best talents. Smart partnering, and the ability to create a partnering culture invigorated by the partnering infrastructure needed to adapt to rapidly changing situations, will enable business leaders to relearn the ancient art of connection and translate it into a modern business model. The Powerhouse Partner Model offers the structure and skills needed to practice focused leadership, build a partnering infrastructure, and develop smart partners, while inspiring employee loyalty and commitment to the vision, mission, and strategic directions of the enterprise. In this book we have shown you in practical ways how to transition your company from a traditional enterprise to a partnering organization.

In a Powerhouse Partner, an abundance mentality rather than a scarcity mentality drives behavior. The catchphrase "together we can get more for everybody" guides behavior more often than "let's hold on to what we've got." If we partner, we get our personal, professional, and organizational needs met—at levels not possible in a competitive environment, not to mention in organization cultures that actively encourage cutthroat behavior among leaders and employees. A Powerhouse Partner tends to attack the marketplace more offensively than a traditional organization, seeing changes—whether economic, social, political, financial, or otherwise—primarily as opportunities for growth and expansion, rather than as threats. A Powerhouse Partner gives people a broad range of accountabilities through strategic directives; connects people through partnering charters; unifies functions by physically positioning departments and people close to each other; and delegates accomplishment of tasks through fewer layers of management and broad spans of control.

A Powerhouse Partner invests enormous resources in finding, hiring, keeping, and growing smart partners: doers, not watchers, who appreciate the potency of partnering and who take personal accountability for delivering on commitments by collaborating with whomever it makes sense to do so, internally and externally. The members of a Powerhouse Partner are recognized and rewarded for displaying the partnering behaviors that deliver results for everyone involved. A Powerhouse Partner replaces the zero-sum game rule book with guidelines anchored in a "we all win" outlook. Smart partners win not only because of what they do, but also because of how they do it.

A Powerhouse Partner aims first at expediting internal alliances among its diverse functions and second at extending the same partnering expertise externally to forge mutually beneficial relationships with customers, suppliers, and other companies. The partnering attribute Self-Disclosure and Feedback enables each of the diverse subcultures of a company to get its own needs met, the fundamental purpose of partnering. Self-disclosure and feedback also help enhance organization openness and thus make it easier for leaders to see the marketplace more quickly, more clearly, and more comprehensively. In a company in which people value and practice the art of self-disclosure and feedback, higher levels of openness become easier to attain.

The attribute Ability to Trust forms the foundation of a work climate in which people know and appreciate the limits of reliability and can be sure that these borders will be respected. Trust is the one characteristic of a partnering culture that is at once both an input into the partnership and an output of the partnership. The people in an organization build trust when they consistently satisfy each other's expectations. Only one experience of betrayal will threaten even the best-crafted partnership. In a Powerhouse Partner the partnering attributes Self-Disclosure and Feedback and Ability to Trust work together to reinforce the organization's foundation for openness.

Like trust, the attribute Future Orientation serves as a kind of lubricant for the organization. Smart partners know themselves well enough to keep from getting trapped in the past, and they trust themselves to make new plans and try innovative approaches. A future orientation helps people and organizations see the possibilities in new situations and approach them with hope and good faith. Creativity at its heart involves seeing the same old things in new ways, letting go of how one has viewed things and done things in the past.

The attribute Comfort with Change enables a Powerhouse Partner to identify obstacles to change, develop strategies for coping with them, and formulate action plans for implementing desired business changes. Survival, reinvigoration, or growth determines why an organization might risk reaching out to form a partnership or strategic alliance. Being comfortable with change helps steady people to take the plunge, to risk belittlement, punishment, even failure. The act of reaching out, of being willing to do something differently, will disrupt the status quo and precipitate change. In a Powerhouse Partner the partnering attributes Future Orientation and Comfort with Change work together to move the organization to the future with creativity.

The attribute Win-Win Orientation means that people use conflict resolution and problem-solving strategies that benefit all parties involved. The people in a Powerhouse Partner lean on the Negotiator style when working together to resolve conflicts. A win-win orientation also forms the heart of marketplaces, the interconnections that give an organization ready access to the capital, competencies, technologies, and other resources it does not possess in-house. Competitive advantage in the twenty-first century will more likely derive from the informal links among marketplaces. Informal exchanges across marketplaces will deliver competent people, information, technology, and materiel to where it is needed, when it is needed, how it is needed, at the price desired.

The final partnering attribute, Comfort with Interdependence, occurs when we have a sense that we're all in this together and we look out for each other's success. When leaders value interdependence, they create an environment that encourages involvement. Moreover, Comfort with Interdependence enables continuity and vibrancy in marketplaces. Interdependence is an active, ongoing process that requires all parties to move from initial independence to vibrant collaboration. Such collaborative strategies require people to forge partnerships in which all sides profit from the success of one another. In a Powerhouse Partner the partnering attributes Win-Win Orientation and Comfort with Interdependence work together to enable the organization to embrace connectivity for agility.

RESILIENCE: THE LIFE JACKET OF A POWERHOUSE PARTNER

From a systems perspective, four characteristics combine to give a Powerhouse Partner the resilience it needs to survive and prosper in the Dual Age of Information and Connections, as shown in Table 12 and described below.

TABLE 12
Resilience of a Powerhouse Partner

DRIVER OR INHIBITOR	WORKFORCE	PRODUCTS & SERVICES	SALES & SERVICE
	SELF-DIRECTING SYSTEM		
Purpose Aimlessness	Spirited Disheartened	Needed/Wanted Unneeded/Unwanted	Enthusiastic Lackluster
	SELF-LEARNING SYSTEM		
Openness Protectionism	Savvy Disoriented	Up-to-date Out-of-date	Knowledgeable Uninformed
	SELF-RENEWING SYSTEM		
Abundance Scarcity	Imaginative Stale	Innovative Boring	Customer focused Product focused
	SELF-REINFORCING SYSTEM		
Connectedness Isolation	Collaborative Combative	High quality Mediocre	Personalized Patronizing

- **Self-Directing.** A Powerhouse Partner knows how to keep its eye on the ball and how to get back on track after a setback.

- **Self-Learning.** A Powerhouse Partner promotes openness and embraces diversity of ideas and approaches for processing information.

- **Self-Renewing.** A Powerhouse Partner approaches the marketplace with an abundance mentality and fosters the organization changes needed to keep pace with the marketplace.

- **Self-Reinforcing.** A Powerhouse Partner understands how to leverage connectedness and appreciates the value of building the relationship skills needed to forge enduring partnerships internally and externally.

The Partnering Organization As a Self-Directing System

As a self-directing system, a Powerhouse Partner knows how to keep its eye on the ball. It can quickly find its bearings and alter course in response to rapid changes in technology, resources, marketplaces, and relationships. Self-direction flows out of grounded, compelling purpose, a driver that results in a spirited workforce that delivers needed and wanted products and services and provides enthusiastic sales and service. The countervailing inhibitor to self-direction is aimlessness, a characteristic that results in a disheartened workforce that delivers unneeded and unwanted products and services and provides lackluster sales and service. In Chapter 3, we emphasized that two powerful forces, ethereal energy and material output, drive organizations, and we presented the Holistic Organization Model as a systematic approach for grasping the interconnected aspects of business strategies and as a mechanism for facilitating alignment across a company.

The *partnering infrastructure component* that plays the largest role in enabling a Powerhouse Partner to be self-directing is the strategic framework (see Chapter 5), for it interconnects the ethereal energies with the material outputs, creating an ongoing, interactive system. A strategic framework starts with a vision statement that describes the desired destiny of the organization—not a point on a timeline, but rather a navigational reference point guiding the business for the long haul. A mission statement describes how an organization will achieve its vision. Strategic directions specify a broad area of organizational focus, things the company needs to do over the next two to three years to achieve its mission.

Human energy is the most powerful energy in any organization. It is an individual's vision, values, passion, and commitment that propel an organization to achieve great things. A leader's most important role is motivating, harnessing, and directing human energy to achieve the objectives of the organization. Leaders must be skilled in leading people by understanding their intrinsic motivators and connecting with their core values. Leaders thereby create the conditions and environment for people to achieve the objectives of the business.

We also discussed in Chapter 4 how creating a Powerhouse Partner requires focused leadership to establish trust and open communication, listen to others' needs, and act on those needs. In the interconnected world of the twenty-first century, organizations can no longer risk alienating either employees or customers by failing to connect with human values. Instead, they must balance the need to accomplish tasks while connecting with people's values, emotions, and desires, their human energy. To accomplish this connection, the first step is to have leaders who create an environment that is open and receptive to partnering with others. Strong leaders build healthy cultures. Cultures by design are deliberate in their development, and this endeavor is where the role of a leader becomes critical. The characteristics outlined in Chapter 4 describe the ideal leader. People look at what leaders do rather than at what they say. They have learned to filter through the rhetoric that passes as the truth to decipher its hidden, convoluted meanings. When people see a contradiction between message and behavior, they tend to dismiss the individual and the message as phony, perhaps hypocritical.

The Partnering Organization As a Self-Learning System

As a self-learning system, a Powerhouse Partner promotes openness and embraces diversity of ideas and approaches for processing information. It rapidly sees and understands changes in technology, marketplaces, and relationships. Self-learning is rooted in openness, a driver that results in a savvy workforce that delivers up-to-date products and services and provides knowledgeable sales and service. The most dangerous inhibitor to self-learning is protectionism, a trait that produces a disoriented workforce that delivers out-of-date products and services and provides uninformed sales and service. Leaders must value openness and practice it among themselves. The executive team must purposefully decide they are going to behave in an open and trusting manner and commit to using the relationship skills of the Six Partnering Attributes. Leaders must hold each other accountable to practice the behaviors to which they have agreed.

The *partnering infrastructure component* that most directly enables a Powerhouse Partner to be self-learning is the partnering network (see Chapter 5). Traditional, hierarchical organization designs institutionalize roadblocks to the flow of information and to the formation of connections, impediments that come as no surprise in that hierarchy functions principally as an instrument of centralized control and risk avoidance. We pointed out that a partnering network is a structure that formally connects an organization's members based on the partnerships and the partnering results most fundamental to implementing the enterprise's strategic framework. Time and distance are heartless, relentless adversaries. A company that aspires to prosper as a Powerhouse Partner has to configure itself so that the members of its most critical partnerships can connect with each other, almost without thinking, as often as they need to. Once again, organizations do not partner; people partner. A partnering network establishes an open platform for instituting and using the market-places and building and using the pathways necessary for rapid, repeatable, direct human interconnections.

In Chapter 8 we stressed that the two *partnering attributes* that form the foundation for organizational openness and self-learning are Self-Disclosure and Feedback and Ability to Trust. Words and actions bond together and result in trust. When we say we are going to do something, and then do it, we build trust. If we don't do it, we dam-age trust. Mastering the art of self-disclosure and feedback is critical to business success. In a business culture, as in life, information flows freely when we feel comfortable and trust those with whom we are communicating. The free flow of information within a business can give a company a powerful competitive edge. But employees will share knowledge and ideas only if leaders have created an internal culture that allows them, in fact encourages them, to do so. If we are uncomfortable and do not trust others, we typically hold information close to the vest and tend not to share as much. The JoHari Window (see Chapter 8) demonstrates how improving the ability to self-disclose and provide feedback can help us explore the unknown, seeing opportunities no one else has seen and improving the bottom line by leveraging these opportunities. Ensuring a free flow of information within an organization requires a systems approach. You can't work on only one problem area—improving employee feedback, for exam-ple—without also working on others, such as building trust and developing comfort with change. Information will stop flowing unless all areas of the system are addressed.

Many executives give lip service to the importance of trust but fail to see a direct connection between their own behavior and the amount of trust people have in their organization. The inability of corporate executives to build trust has a more far-reaching impact than just its effect on their immediate employees. This mistrust of business leaders translates directly to investor reluctance, which then denies businesses access to the capital they need to grow, which then hurts their employees and the overall economy. A direct correlation exists between how employees view their company and how customers and stockholders view it. Once leaders have lost the confidence of employees, that negative energy has a measurable impact on the messages employees—and especially frontline employees—deliver to customers, the community at large, and stockholders. You can measure trust just like you measure product quality or customer service excellence. When used properly, a trust indicator can let you know in advance if something is weakening trust in your business. This tracking of trust is a small investment in maintaining morale, keeping information lines open, and maintaining your good reputation in the marketplace. When building a partnering culture, leaders must start with a foundation for openness.

The Partnering Organization As a Self-Renewing System

As a self-renewing system, a Powerhouse Partner approaches the marketplace with an abundance mentality and fosters the organization changes needed to keep pace with the marketplace. A partnering organization swiftly adapts products and services to leverage changes in technology, marketplaces, and relationships. An organization has little chance of being self-renewing without an abundance mentality, a driver that results in an imaginative workforce that delivers innovative products and services and provides problem-focused sales and service. More common in organizations is a scarcity mentality, an inhibitor that results in a stale workforce that delivers boring products and services and provides product-focused sales and service. A Powerhouse Partner focuses on its vision for the future and sets expectations for employees with that vision in mind. It also requires leaders to be open and accepting of new ideas. A hallmark of effective leadership is the ability to introduce required change in the organization. The industrial economy was based on the concept of scarcity and the conservation of material goods, resources of both the material and human varieties. Information becomes more valuable as it becomes abundant, and as it spreads, it can morph into something new. Both information and connections appreciate as organization assets.

The *partnering infrastructure component* that most directly enables a Powerhouse Partner to be self-renewing is the hiring of people with partnering competencies. People build an organization's culture through what they believe and what they value and how they treat each other, partners, and customers. To build a Powerhouse Partner, the leaders of a company must know what kinds of behaviors expedite and propel human connections and, by extension, which competencies drive partnering behaviors. In the twenty-first century, smart partnering is emerging as one of the preeminent competencies needed for outstanding job performance, and hiring people with partnering competencies will accelerate the building of a Powerhouse Partner. In Chapter 6 we outlined a suite of six partnering competencies with sample behavioral indicators; offered the Partnering Interview as an innovative, empirical approach for determining the breadth and depth of a job candidate's partnering competencies; and provided a Partnering Interview Plan with sample questions as a protocol for conducting team Partnering Interviews. Partnering with colleagues to conduct a Partnering Interview has a substantive advantage over conducting only one-on-one behavioral interviews.

In Chapter 9 we underscored that the two *partnering attributes* driving a Powerhouse Partner to move to the future with creativity and remain self-renewing are Future Orientation and Comfort with Change. Living in the future is one of the most difficult behavior changes leaders must undergo if they are to rewire their business cultures for the Dual Age of Information and Connections. Having a past orientation—especially within the ranks of leaders—is one reason that organizations have difficulty innovating. As a leader, when you speak about the future in terms that betray a past orientation, you're giving people conflicting messages. To make the transition from a past to a future orientation, those who are resistant to change must learn to be comfortable doing things differently, to challenge their belief system, and to plan for the future. When using future-oriented language, you must be careful to differentiate the person from the outcome of the past activity (see Chapter 9). Continuing to focus on errors and not trying to remove obstacles to success is a hallmark of a past orientation. You can start the reorientation of your culture by changing your language.

All change is personal, especially when it is happening to you. The potential for a change event to damage trust and create win-lose situations is high. Partnering cultures follow four simple steps to ensure that when the change event is completed, people still trust leaders and feel like everyone has won:

- Get clear on the case for change

- Align the change with the strategic framework

- Integrate the change into the organization structure

- Communicate, communicate, communicate

Leaders need to be clear about the nature of the change event occurring. Trying to implement change that is inconsistent with the values and strategic direction of an organization can be devastating. When planning for a change event, be sure that you enlist representatives from each department or team in the business, share the planned upcoming change, and talk about the impact the change will have on each group. Put together teams of people to develop win-win outcomes and plans to mitigate any destructive backlash or sabotage that may appear. Leaders must organize formal and informal communication pathways and connections focused solely on the change event. The more two-way dialogues between leaders and employees, the higher the likelihood of a successful change. Powerhouse Partners know that during a time of transition, the key to success is letting go of fear.

The Partnering Organization As a Self-Reinforcing System

As a self-reinforcing system, a Powerhouse Partner understands how to leverage connectedness and appreciates the value of building the relationship skills needed to forge enduring partnerships internally and externally. Smart partners quickly make the personal and business connections required to deploy new products and services and thus enable their enterprise to profit from changes in technology, marketplaces, and relationships. An organization becomes self-reinforcing principally through connectedness, a driver that results in a collaborative workforce that delivers high-quality products and services and provides personalized sales and service. The organization characteristic that will undermine self-reinforcement most severely is isolation, an inhibitor that results in a combative workforce that delivers mediocre products and services and provides patronizing sales and service. People working for a Powerhouse Partner know how to manage their emotions, defer self-gratification for the good of others, and negotiate successful outcomes. Leaders are willing to rely on others for success. Organizations and the level of information needed to operate them are far too complex for any one individual to act in isolation. Leaders know how to delegate and hold others accountable for results.

The *partnering infrastructure component* that most directly enables a Powerhouse Partner to be self-reinforcing is keeping and growing smart partners (see Chapter 7). People add value whether by serving customers, building or selling products, or running the business. In the emerging information and connection economy, interpersonal relationships act as transmission conduits, as connectors. When employees are treated as trusted partners in an enterprise, they are freed up to pool their collective creative energies for the benefit of the business as a whole. More connections produce more good ideas; more good ideas result in more great ideas; and more great ideas deliver extraordinary innovation. Smart partners drive creativity by increasing the frequency, frankness, and fruitfulness of interpersonal connections, dialogue, and collaboration. Leaders who want to build a Powerhouse Partner must proactively learn, apply, and refine a robust set of partnering skills, and they must ensure that employees build the relationship skills needed to execute against the company's strategic framework.

In Chapter 7 we made three suggestions for how an organization's leaders can keep and grow smart partners:

- Build loyalty and a sense of duty

- Coach people to grow informal communication networks (pathways)

- Strengthen relationship skills: the diversity of management skills of leaders and the partnering skills of employees

If you invest energy in employees' loyalty, they in turn will provide added value. If you do not invest in employees, ignore them, or abuse them, the opposite will occur. Establishing a coaching and mentoring program to accelerate the cultivation of informal communication networks is an important step in creating a Powerhouse Partner. The particular kind of diversity that twenty-first-century leaders must be able to manage is the diversity of ideas and opinions and how people express those ideas. People in different parts of an enterprise are likely to need different kinds of relationship skills. Neither an organization's leaders nor its employees will acquire them by osmosis, by accident, or by divine intervention. These relationship skills must be built by design.

In Chapter 10 we underscored that the two *partnering attributes* driving a Powerhouse Partner to embrace connectivity for agility and remain self-reinforcing are Win-Win Orientation and Comfort with Interdependence. Partnering is an unnatural act for most of us—the relationship skills required for being a great partner and building a partnering culture are often counterintuitive. Businesses that have invested in learning smart partnering skills and in creating a partnering culture have the relationship skills needed to weather major marketplace changes without fear. Having a culture that is grounded in trust, able to communicate, and focused on the future will give your enterprise a competitive advantage. A fundamental correlation exists between satisfied employees and satisfied customers. The key to any leader's success is striking a balance between getting results and satisfying employees' needs. Use a win-win orientation and you may be surprised to discover that a conflict between achieving results and building a loyal workforce is not inevitable. The only conflict resolution style that is designed for producing a win-win outcome is the Negotiator style. The process is time consuming, but the alternative, creating losers on your team, will ultimately cause you to waste more time and resources than spending the energy up front and resolving the issue.

To survive in the interconnected world of the twenty-first century, you have to make sure that you succeed and that your partners and colleagues succeed. Your ability to be comfortable with such a high level of interdependence depends on your capacity to master the Six Partnering Attributes, since each links with the others to form a partnering culture. In the Dual Age of Information and Connections, businesses cannot afford to waste any human resource. Interdependence must be a part of the culture and embedded in every action we take.

Be a Powerhouse Partner

In the Dual Age of Information and Connections, task achievement alone will no longer propel an organization—or its stock valuation—to where its stakeholders demand that it go. Creating the innovation, business relationships, and value needed to move a company to the next level requires a focused effort on harnessing and releasing human potential and creativity. In most organizations, the worse things get operationally or financially, the more people tend to hunker down and just do things. Building relationships, communicating needs, and doing it right the first time result in less rework and higher-quality output, faster and cheaper. Smart partners know that sharing information is the currency of success and that building a collaborative culture to enable that to happen is the next logical step.

To accomplish this goal, an organization needs to have in place a process that enables everyone to slow down under stress and be guided by leaders grounded in the personal mastery of being smart partners. Ideally, the organization infrastructure includes a grounded, compelling strategic framework, aligned strategies and tactics, agreements on priorities and allocation of resources, the right people with the right skills in the right jobs, and reward and compensation systems that drive the right behaviors. An organization must have a plan in place to help its people continue to hone their partnering skills, with the goal of making them smarter partners.

The first step in building a partnering culture needs to be taken by an organization's executive leaders. Leaders must move beyond intellectually understanding partnering behaviors into living partnering behaviors everyday. The Six Partnering Attributes create a language that enables team members to communicate better with each other about which behaviors are productive and which are counterproductive.

The second step in creating a partnering culture is ensuring that the organization's infrastructure supports a collaborative culture. People will do what they are paid to do, not what leaders preach that they expect them to do. If you want collaborative behavior, you must balance the reward for both collaborative behavior and individual contribution.

Once leaders have attained personal mastery using the Six Partnering Attributes, and once organization structures and processes have been put into place to support the use of these attributes, employees must be trained in their use to accomplish their work tasks. This continuous strengthening of partnering skills creates a self-reinforcing network and embeds the partnering language and behaviors deeper and deeper within the organization.

Creating a Powerhouse Partner using the Powerhouse Partner Model requires that you invest time, money, and energy in both achieving tasks and in building relationships. This task–relationship balance constitutes a central partnering force that must always be in the forefront of a leader's mind. The act of transforming an organization culture, a paradox in itself, is messy and complex and requires leaders to exemplify their strongest relationship abilities. Leaders must push the boundaries of patience with people. Unfortunately for many businesses, it's at this point that every instinct signals people to hunker down and get back to task at the expense of the relationship. Ethereal energies result directly from a leader's ability to create an organizational environment that supports and encourages human achievement. Material output directly reflects the ethereal energy within an organization. Although the short-term effect of an imbalance between achieving tasks and building relationships may seem insignificant to leaders, the long-term impact on a business can be deadly.

Day by day, leaders must demonstrate the partnering behaviors needed to create cultures that thrive on open, positive communication and win-win problem-solving and conflict resolution strategies— cultures that are future focused, adaptable, and interdependent. The kind of organization culture that made the developed world an industrial powerhouse over the past half-century will not sustain businesses in the next economic age. In the Dual Age of Information and Connections, businesses operate on fundamentally different principles from those of the Industrial Age. Imagine harnessing the brilliance of the workforce. Imagine learning from each other. Imagine being an innovation factory, turning out new and exciting ideas and concepts on a regular basis. Imagine having a workforce that is not just loyal, but feels a sense of duty to the success of the organization. These aspirations are not just the compilations of an executive wish list. They are the goals that must be reached to become a Powerhouse Partner in the Dual Age of Information and Connections.

Bibliography

Ainsworth-Land, George T. *Grow or Die: The Unifying Principle of Transformation.* Reissue. New York: John Wiley & Sons, 1986. (Original edition by George T. Lock Land, 1973; see also below, George Land.)

Bloom, Howard. *Global Brain: The Evolution of Mass Mind from the Big Bang to the 21st Century.* New York: John Wiley & Sons, 2000.

Boulton, Richard E. S., Barry D. Libert, and Steven M. Samek, *Cracking the Value Code.* New York: HarperBusiness, 2000.

Boyington, Gregory "Pappy." *Baa Baa Black Sheep.* New York: Bantam Books, 1977.

Childre, Doc, and Bruce Cryer. *From Chaos to Coherence: Advancing Emotional and Organizational Intelligence Through Inner Quality Management.* Boston: Butterworth-Heinemann, 1999.

Churchill, Winston. *My Early Life: 1874–1904.* With an introduction by William Manchester. New York: A Touchstone Book: Simon & Schuster, 1958.

Csikszentmihalyi, Mihaly. *Creativity: Flow and the Psychology of Discovery and Invention.* New York: HarperCollins, 1996.

Dent, Stephen M. *Partnering Intelligence: Creating Value for Your Business by Building Strong Alliances.* 2d ed. Palo Alto, CA: Davies-Black Publishing, 2004.

Dent, Stephen M., James H. Krefft, and Susan Schaefer. "Driving Growth Through a Holistic Strategic Framework: A Telecommunications Company Case Study." In Lyle Yorks, *Strategic Human Resource Development.* Mason, OH: South-Western, 2004.

Dent, Stephen M., and Sandra M. Naiman. *The Partnering Intelligence Fieldbook: Tools and Techniques for Building Strong Alliances for Your Business.* Palo Alto, CA: Davies-Black Publishing, 2002.

de Waal, Frans B. M. *Tree of Origin: What Primate Behavior Can Tell Us About Human Social Evolution.* Cambridge, MA: Harvard University Press, 2001.

de Waal, Frans B. M., and Peter L. Tyack. *Animal Social Complexity: Intelligence, Culture, and Individualized Societies.* Cambridge, MA: Harvard University Press, 2003.

Dugatkin, Lee Alan. *The Imitation Factor: Evolution Beyond the Gene.* New York: Simon & Schuster, 2001.

Dunne, John S. *Time and Myth.* New York: Doubleday, 1973.

Erasmus, Desiderius. *The Praise of Folly.* Trans. John Wilson (1668). Ann Arbor: University of Michigan Press, 1958.

Evans, Philip, and Thomas S. Wurster. *Blown to Bits: How the New Economics of Information Transforms Strategy.* Boston: Harvard Business School Press, 2000.

Foot, M. R. D. *SOE: An Outline History of the Special Operations Executive, 1940–1946.* With an introduction by David Stafford. London: Pimlico, 1999.

Friedman, Brian, James Hatch, and David M. Walker. *Delivering on the Promise: How to Attract, Manage, and Retain Human Capital.* New York: Free Press, 1998.

Galbraith, Jay R. *Designing Organizations: An Executive Briefing on Strategy, Structure, and Process.* San Francisco: Jossey-Bass, 1995.

Garten, Jeffrey E. *World View: Global Strategies for the New Economy.* Boston: Harvard Business School Press, 2000.

Garvin, David. *Learning in Action: A Guide to Putting Learning Organizations to Work.* Boston: Harvard Business School Press, 2000.

Goffee, Rob, and Gareth Jones. *The Character of a Corporation: How Your Company's Culture Can Make or Break Your Business.* New York: HarperBusiness, 1998.

Hallowell, Edward M. *Connect.* New York: Pantheon Books, 1999.

Hamel, Gary. *Leading the Revolution.* Boston: Harvard Business School Press, 2000.

Hammarskjöld, Dag. *Markings.* Trans. Leif Sjöberg and W. H. Auden. New York: Alfred A. Knopf, 1976.

Hammer, Michael, and Steven A. Stanton. *The Reengineering Revolution: A Handbook.* New York: HarperBusiness, 1995.

Hammer, Michael. *Beyond Reengineering: How the Process-Centered Organization Is Changing Our Work and Our Lives.* New York: HarperBusiness, 1996.

Howe, Neil, and William Strauss. *Millennials Rising: The Next Great Generation.* New York: Vintage, 2000.

Kaplan, Robert S., and David P. Norton. *The Strategy-Focused Organization: How Balance Scorecard Companies Thrive in the New Business Environment.* Boston: Harvard Business School Press, 2001.

Katzenbach, John R. *Peak Performance: Aligning the Hearts and Minds of Your Employees.* Boston: Harvard Business School Press, 2000.

Kennedy, Allan A. *The End of Shareholder Value: Corporations at the Crossroads.* Cambridge, MA: Perseus Books, 2000.

Krefft, James H. "Linking People and Processes." In *ASQ's 53rd Annual Quality Congress Proceedings,* pp. 454–460. Milwaukee: ASQ, 1999.

Krefft, James H., and Lyle Yorks. "Driving Performance Improvement by Hard-Wiring People to Core Business Processes: A Financial Services Firm Case Study." In Lyle Yorks, *Human Resource Development in Organizations: Building Strategic Capability Through Learning.* Mason, OH: South-Western, 2004.

Land, George, and Beth Jarman. *Breakpoint and Beyond: Mastering the Future—Today.* New York: HarperBusiness, 1992. (See also above, George T. Ainsworth-Land.)

Levine, Rick, Christopher Locke, Doc Searls, and David Weinberger. *The Cluetrain Manifesto: The End of Business As Usual.* Cambridge, MA: Perseus Books, 1999.

Litwin, George H., and Robert A. Stringer, Jr. *Motivation and Organizational Climate.* Boston: Harvard University, 1968.

Longstreet, James. *From Manassas to Appomattox: Memoirs of the Civil War in America.* 1896. Reprint, with an introduction by Jeffry D. Wert, New York: Da Capo Press, 1992.

MacDonald, Charles B. *Company Commander.* Washington, DC: Infantry Journal Press, 1947; reprint, Short Hills, NJ: Burford Books, 1999.

Moore, Geoffrey A. *Living on the Fault Line: Managing for Shareholder Value in the Age of the Internet.* New York: HarperBusiness, 2000.

More, St. Thomas. *Utopia.* Ed. and trans. Edward Surtz. New Haven, CT: Yale University Press, 1964.

Ornstein, Robert E. *Multimind.* Boston: Houghton Mifflin, 1986.

Petzinger, Thomas, Jr. *The New Pioneers: The Men and Women Who Are Transforming the Workplace and Marketplace.* New York: Simon & Schuster, 1999.

Pfeffer, Jeffery, and Charles A. O'Reilly, III. *Hidden Value: How Great Companies Achieve Extraordinary Results with Ordinary People.* Boston: Harvard Business School Press, 2000.

Pitera, Joanne. "Driving Transformational Change Through the Organization." Chap. 13 in *Lessons in Cultural Change: The Utility Industry Experience,* ed. Philip R. Theibert. Arlington, VA: Public Utilities Reports, 1994.

Schein, Edgar H. *The Corporate Culture Survival Guide: Sense and Nonsense About Culture Change.* San Francisco: Jossey-Bass, 1999.

Schneider, William E. *The Reengineering Alternative: A Plan for Making Your Current Culture Work.* New York: Irwin Professional Publishing, 1994.

Smart, Bradford D. *Topgrading: How Leading Companies Win by Hiring, Coaching, and Keeping the Best People.* Paramus, NJ: Prentice Hall, 1999.

Teilhard de Chardin, Pierre. *Christianity and Evolution.* New York: Harcourt Brace Jovanovich, 1964.

Thomas, K. W., and R. H. Kilmann, *Thomas-Kilmann Conflict Mode Instrument.* Palo Alto, CA: XICOM, 1974.

Thoreau, Henry David. *Walden; or, Life in the Woods.* With an introduction by Norman Holmes Pearson (1948). New York: Holt, Rinehart and Winston, 1965.

Yorks, Lyle. "Applying Human Resource Technologies in Support of Strategically Driven Transformational Change at Thermo King." Chap. 2 in *HR to the Rescue: Case Studies of HR Solutions to Business Challenges,* ed. Edward M. Mone and Manuel London. Houston: Gulf, 1998.

Yorks, Lyle. *Strategic Human Resource Development.* Mason, OH: South-Western, 2004.

Zimmerman, John, Sr. *The Culture of Success: Building a Sustained Competitive Advantage by Living Your Corporate Beliefs.* New York: McGraw-Hill, 1997.

Index

Ability to Trust: behavioral indicators for, 99; characteristics of, 29; definition of, 56, 96; description of, 206; leader's role in, 32; as partnering competency, 96; self-assessments, 153–154; Self-Disclosure and Feedback and, 135–136. *See also* trust

abundance mentality, 160, 205, 212

accountability: for change, 180; as competency, 91; definition of, 91; description of, 55, 65, 205; questions for evaluating, 92

achieving results, 55–56

actions: loyalty-promoting, 120, 122–123; motivation of, 54–55

adjuster of change, 174–175

Age of Enlightenment, 2

agility of partnering culture, 35

alliances, 3

assumptions, 172

behavior(s): collaborative, 44; of leaders, 18–19; of loyal employees, 120; in partnering organization, 24–25; trust-related, 151

behavioral indicators: for Ability to Trust, 99; for Comfort with Change, 99; for Comfort with Interdependence, 99; competencies and, 90–93; definition of, 90; for Future Orientation, 99; for Self-Disclosure and Feedback, 99, for Win-Win Orientation, 99

behavioral interviews, 86

change: ability to, 157–158; accountability for, 180; adjusters of, 174–175; case study of, 176–178; chaos and, 180–181; clarity of reasons for, 176–178; comfort with. *See* Comfort with Change; communication about, 179–180; coping with, 30, 97; description of, 214; embracing of, 163; future orientation and, 173–176; initiators of, 174; management of, 165; organization structure and, 178–179; partnering for, 176–181; past orientation effects on, 163–165; perceived need for, 97; rejecters of,

change, *continued*
175–176; strategic framework aligned with, 178
change agents, 174–176
chaos, 180–181
coaching, 124–126, 216
collaborative behaviors, 44
collaborative culture, 5, 218
Comfort with Change: behavioral indicators for, 99; characteristics of, 30; definition of, 56, 97; description of, 206–207, 213; leader's role in, 33; as partnering competency, 97
Comfort with Interdependence: behavioral indicators for, 99; characteristics of, 31; definition of, 56, 97; description of, 207, 216; leader's role in, 33; as partnering competency, 97–98
command and control management style, 160–161, 184
communication: behavioral indicators for, 90–91; about change, 179–180; conflict resolution and, 191; culture and, 133–136; environment for, 122; language for, 166; mistrust effects on, 152; with passion, 200–201
communication networks, 124–126, 216
competencies: accountability, 91; behavioral indicators and, 90–93; communication, 90–91; core, 94; drive to win, 91; objectives achieved using, 89–90; purpose of, 89; technical expertise, 91. *See also* partnering competencies
competency, 89

competency-based assessment, 85, 88–89. *See also* job competence assessment
competency model, 92–93
Compromiser style of conflict resolution, 189
conflict: description of, 164–165; diversity and, 126; fight-or-flight response to, 192, 194; information sharing effects of, 147–148; management of, 187–199
conflict resolution: collaborative approach to, 197; communication and, 191; Compromiser style of, 189; description of, 188; Evader style of, 188; Fighter style of, 189; Harmonizer style of, 190; leadership responsibilities, 198; Negotiator style of, 190–191, 195, 198, 217; Win-Win Orientation. *See* Win-Win Orientation; win-win outcomes, 190
connectivity: Age of Enlightenment effects on, 2; history of, 1; human survival and, 1, 203; importance of, 203; Industrial Age effects on, 2
controlled production, 159–160
core competencies, 94
core human values, 127–129
cosourcing, 35
creativity: description of, 37; encouraging of, 201; energy created by, 201; language and, 171; mistrust effects on, 152; of partnering culture, 34–35; smart partnering effects on, 6, 130, 215

cultural transmission, 12–13
culture: communication and,
133–136; diversity-based
differences, 129; fight-or-flight
response effects on, 194; foundation of, 6–7; information-
sharing, 146–149; loyalty valued
in, 119; of organization. *See*
organization culture; partnering. *See* partnering culture;
survival and, 11–12
culture by design, 4, 16–17, 31,
129, 204
culture by evolution, 4, 16–17,
31, 129

date copying, 13
decision making, 129, 187
diversity: building of, 201; conflict
and, 126; of core human values,
127–129; and cultural differences,
129–130; of decision-making
styles, 129; description of, 126;
and information-sharing differences, 129; of opinions and
ideas, 128
drive to win: definition of, 91;
questions for evaluating, 92
Dual Age of Information and
Connections: controlled vs.
open production in, 159–160;
description of, 3–4, 7, 41, 49;
Industrial Age vs., 159; information's value in, 148; leaders
in, 186; Powerhouse Partner
in, 65; principles of, 64; scarcity
mentality vs. abundance mentality, 160

employees: coaching and mentoring
program benefits for, 127;
communication with, 191;
compensating of, 116; leadership and, 185; morale of, 185;
needs of, 187; with partnering
competencies, 86–87; sense
of duty among, 123–124; tools
and training for, 117–119; trust
of, 152, 215; valuation of, 117
environment: behavioral adaptations to, 10; future orientation
view of, 166; leader's influence
on, 49, 135; of open communication, 122; of organizations,
9–10, 49; past orientation view
of, 166; well-being effects of, 10
ethereal energy: definition of, 46;
description of, 218; examples
of, 47–48
Evader style of conflict resolution,
188

fear, 15
feedback: importance of, 95; about
trust, 154–155
Fighter style of conflict resolution,
189
fight-or-flight response, 192, 194
focused leadership: definition of,
52; description of, 5; foundation of, 52; and inspiring of
vision, 53–54; and motivation
of action, 54–55; partnering
culture and, 43; personal
mastery and, 52–53
Future Orientation: assessment
of, 167–169; behavioral
indicators for, 99; change
and, 173–176; characteristics
of, 29–30; definition of, 56;
description of, 206, 213;
difficulties associated with,

Future Orientation, *continued*
171–172; environment viewed
from, 166; examples of, 172;
language associated with, 170;
leader's role in, 32; learned
nature of, 173; as partnering
competency, 96–97; in partnering culture, 34; past orientation
transition to, 214

global pathways, 78

Harmonizer style of conflict
resolution, 190
hierarchical organizations, 160, 211
Holistic Organization Model,
46–47, 208
hope, 122
human energy, 46–47, 209–210
human values, 127–129

ideas, diversity of, 128
Industrial Age: characteristics
of, 159–162; description of,
2; Dual Age of Information
and Connections vs., 159
information: as commodity, 161;
exponential nature of, 147;
material vs., 161–162
Information Age, 3
information sharing: competitive
benefits of, 147; conflict effects
on, 147–148; culture of,
146–149; description of, 129,
211; internal partnerships for,
148–149; systems approach
to, 148–149; trust and, 138
initiator of change, 174
innovation: description of, 15, 141;
past orientation effects on, 164

inspiring of vision, 53–54
institutionalized partnering, 83–84
interdependence: comfort with.
See Comfort with Interdependence; description of, 31, 98,
199–200; steps involved in,
200–202; valuing of, 207
internal partnerships, 148–149
interviews: behavioral, 86; Partnering. *See* Partnering Interview

job competence assessment: "academically rigorous" form of, 88;
definition of, 88; premise of, 88
job description, 71–72, 82
job design: definition of, 66;
innovation in, 71; partnering
and, 67, 69–71
job evaluation system, 69–70
job profile, 93
job spec, 67, 69
JoHari Window, 137–140, 211

knowledge sharing, 146
knowledge transference, 163, 171

language: communication uses of,
166; energy created by, 171;
future-oriented, 170; past-
oriented, 170
leaders: accountability of, 180;
actions of, 51; behaviors of,
18–19, 219; case study of, 57,
112–114; challenges for, 186;
decision making by, 187;
in Dual Age of Information
and Connections, 186;
environment created by, 49,
135; expectations of, 186;
historical examples of,

134–135; inspiring of vision by, 53–54; loyalty promoted by, 116–117; mistrust of, 149, 212; motivation of action by, 54–55; organization culture affected by, 14–17, 49, 203–204; Partnering Attributes of. *See* Partnering Attributes; partnering organi-zation role of, 32–33; results achieved by, 55–56; trust building and, 149
leadership: conflict resolution responsibilities of, 198; effective, 213; employees and, 185; focused. *See* focused leadership; foundation of, 52; managing a business vs., 45–50; past orientation and, 173; relationship skills for, 45
leading by example: description of, 18–19; in partnering organization, 31–33
linear/sequential mind-set, 161
loyalty: actions for promoting, 120, 122–123; behaviors associated with, 120; benefits of, 120; building of, 118–119, 120, 122–123, 131, 216; case study of, 119–120, 121–122; growth of, 115–116; leader's role in promoting, 115–116; tools and training for maintaining, 117–119; trust and, 122

management: command and control style of, 160–161; leadership vs., 45–50
marketplaces, 76–77
material output: definition of, 46; examples of, 48–49

mentoring, 124–126
mission statement, 61
motivation of action, 54–55

Negotiator style of conflict resolution, 190–191, 195, 198, 217
network-structured organizations, 160

openness: foundation of, 34, 202; of partnering culture, 34; promotion of, 210; reinforcing of, 155–156; self-learning and, 210
open production, 159–160
opinions, diversity of, 128
organic networks, 36
organic/neural mind-set, 161
organization: coaching and mentoring program benefits for, 127; command and control management style in, 160–161; conflict within, 147–148; controlled vs. open production in, 159–160; description of, 9; design of, 79; environment of, 9–10; hierarchical, 160, 211; human energy in, 46–47, 209–210; information sharing by, 41; linear/sequential, 161; network structure in, 160; organic/neural, 161; partnering. *See* partnering organization; scarcity mentality vs. abundance mentality in, 160; traditional, 22–25; word origin of, 59
organization culture: bottom-line business results affected by, 13–14, 203; building of,

organization culture, *continued*
39–40, 85; characteristics of,
11; definition of, 11; elements
of, 11, 46; failure of, 40–41;
leaders' effect on, 14–17, 49,
203–204; marketplaces, 76–77;
pathways, 77–78; power of,
40–41; risk taking and, 15;
sources of, 46; transforming
of, 45, 157–163, 218
organization design, 66–67
organization structure: change
integrated into, 178–179;
description of, 65–67, 83–84
orientation: assumptions' effect
on, 172; future. *See* Future
Orientation; past. *See* past
orientation
outsourcing, 35

partnering: characteristics of, 69;
with colleague, 130; history
of, 1–2, 9; importance of, 3;
information gained from, 69;
institutionalized, 83–84; job
design and, 67, 69–71; as job
evaluation factor, 71; relationships gained from, 69; smart,
3–4; unnatural nature of,
183–184, 216
Partnering Attributes: Ability to
Trust. *See* Ability to Trust;
characteristics of, 27; Comfort
with Change. *See* Comfort
with Change; Comfort with
Interdependence. *See* Comfort
with Interdependence;
description of, 43, 211; Future
Orientation. *See* Future
Orientation; list of, 4–5, 26;
Self-Disclosure and Feedback.

See Self-Disclosure and Feedback; Win-Win Orientation.
See Win-Win Orientation
partnering competencies: Ability
to Trust, 96; case study of,
100–101; Comfort with
Change, 97; Comfort with
Interdependence, 97–98;
description of, 86; discussion
about, 88–90; Future Orientation, 96–97; hiring people with,
86–87, 109, 213; Self-Disclosure and Feedback, 94–95;
Win-Win Orientation, 95.
See also competencies
partnering culture: agility of, 35;
benefits of, 33–36, 185; building of, 218–219; case study
of, 62–64; collaboration in,
26; communication's role in,
179–180; creating of, 4–5, 37;
creativity of, 34–35; definition
of, 162; description of, 25–26,
72; focused leadership for, 43;
future orientation of, 34; infrastructure for, 44, 60–64; openness of, 34; overview of, 4–5;
purpose of, 25; resiliency of,
35–36; strategic framework for,
60–64, 178, 209
partnering infrastructure, 209, 211,
213, 215
Partnering Interview: case study
of, 105–106; conducting of, 98,
100–102, 107–110; definition
of, 98; description of, 86,
109–110; focus of, 109; format
of, 102; inquiry strategies used
in, 107; interviewer training for,
101–102; plan for, 104, 110;
questioning pitfalls in, 108;

questioning techniques used in, 107–108; structure of, 103; team members, 103–104; tips for, 107–110; what to probe in, 109

partnering network: brainstorming options for, 81; building of, 74–75; case study of, 79; description of, 72, 211; design criteria for, 78, 80–81; implementation of, 83; marketplaces, 76–77; pathways, 77–78; steps involved in, 80–83

partnering organization: behaviors in, 24–25; building of, 60, 93–94; case studies of, 68–70; characteristics of, 22–25; creating of, 84; description of, 21; leader's role in, 32–33; leading by example in, 31–33; partnering competencies used to build, 94; as self-directing system, 208–210; as self-learning system, 210–212; as self-reinforcing system, 215–217; as self-renewing system, 212–214

partnering profile, 71–73

partnering quotient, 26

Partnering Quotient Assessment, 94

partnering summary, 72, 74–75

past orientation: assessment of, 167–169; change and, 163–165; definition of, 30; environment viewed from, 166; examples of, 172; future orientation transition of, 213; future orientation vs., 96; innovation effects, 164; "knowledge transference" and, 163; language associated with, 170; leader's focus on, 34; leadership's effect on, 173

pathways, 77–78

personal mastery, 52–53, 218

Powerhouse Partner: abundance mentality of, 205; benefits of, 64–65; characteristics of, 204–207; description of, 8; in Dual Age of Information and Connections, 65; how to become, 217–219; resilience of, 208–219; smart partners valued by, 205

Powerhouse Partner Model: benefits of, 205; description of, 41–43, 218; focused leadership. *See* focused leadership; introduction to, 5–7; relationship building and, 44–45; schematic diagram of, 42; task achievement and, 44–45

protectionism, 210

rejecters of change, 175–176

relationships: building of, 44–45; leadership and, 45; and trust, 136, 150–151

relationship skills, 126–130, 162, 184

resiliency of partnering culture, 35–36

results, achieving of, 55–56, 186

risk taking, 15

scarcity mentality, 160, 212–213

self-assessments: Future Orientation, 167–169; past orientation, 167–169; trust, 153–154; Win-Win Orientation, 192–193

self-directing system, 208–210

Self-Disclosure and Feedback: Ability to Trust and, 135–136; assessment of, 142–143;

Self-Disclosure and Feedback, *continued*
behavioral indicators for, 99; business success and, 136–137; characteristics of, 27–28; definition of, 56, 94–95; description of, 206; JoHari Window, 137–140, 211; leader's role in, 32; as partnering competency, 94–95; profile, 143–145
self-learning, 210–212
self-reinforcing system, 215–217
self-reliance, 36
self-renewing system, 212–214
sense of duty, 123–124
small-mindedness, 141
smart partnering: benefits of, 205; case study of, 140; creativity increased by, 6, 130, 215; description of, 3–4; job performance and, 86
smart partners: finding of, 86; growth of, 115–116, 130–131, 215–216; hiring of, 109–110; loyalty of. *See* loyalty; maintaining of, 130–131; Powerhouse Partner valuation of, 205
steering committee, 81
strategic direction, 61–62
strategic framework, 60–64, 178, 209
subcultures, 11

task elements of trust, 136, 150
task–relationship balance, 44–45, 218
teamwork, 199
technical expertise: definition of, 91; questions for evaluating, 92

trailblazing, 53
trust: behaviors associated with, 151; building of, 43, 94, 96, 149–150, 154–155, 201; communication and, 152; competencies for, 150; definition of, 29, 151; employee, 152; feedback about, 154–155; importance of, 154, 212; indicators of, 152, 212; JoHari Window, 137–140; loyalty and, 122; measurement of, 151–152; relationship component of, 136, 150–151; self-assessments, 153–154; self-disclosure and, 94; task component of, 136, 150; types of, 136. *See also* Ability to Trust
trustworthiness, 153

vision: clarity of, 200; inspiring of, 53–54; objectives aligned with, 200
vision statement, 61, 165

win-lose approach, 161
win-win approach, 161
Win-Win Orientation: behavioral indicators for, 99; characteristics of, 28–29; creation of, 202; definition of, 56; description of, 207, 216; indicator of, 199; leader's role in, 32; measurement of, 198–199; outcomes of, 28; as partnering competency, 95; self-assessments, 192–193, 196–197; steps for achieving, 197–198; team profile, 194–195
"workplace rationalism," 2